# Kidsafe

*Everything
You Need to
Know to Make
Your Child's
Environment Safe*

## Rae Tyson

TIMES BOOKS

RANDOM HOUSE

Library of Congress Cataloging-in-Publication Data

Tyson, Rae.
    Kidsafe : everything you need to know to make your child's
environment safe / Rae Tyson. — 1st ed.
        p.    cm.
    Includes index.
    ISBN 0-8129-2414-2 (trade paperback)
    1. Pediatric toxicology.   2. Children's accidents—Prevention.
I. Title.
RA1225.T97   1995
615.9'083—dc20                                        94–46665

Manufactured in the United States of America

9   8   7   6   5   4   3   2

First Edition

To my wife, Joan, for her patience
and to my children, Mariah and
Peter. Without them I never
would have understood why the
health and safety of our kids is so
important. And to my dad and
sister, Barb, for their unwavering
support.

# ACKNOWLEDGMENTS

I'd like to thank my Times Books editor, Elizabeth Rapoport, for allowing me to develop her original concept and to all the concerned parents who made me realize why the book was so necessary. I also am indebted to my editors at *USA Today,* who have entrusted me with one of the best jobs in journalism, and to all the scientists who have over the years taken the time to help me better understand the intricacies of environmental science. Dora McKelvey-Goryl deserves credit for her superb illustrations. And finally, a special thanks to the Society of Environmental Journalists, an organization that has elevated the professionalism of environmental journalism worldwide.

# FOREWORD

After nearly two decades as an environmental writer, I've come to expect a strong reaction whenever one of my news stories reports some new environmental risk affecting children. Parents are concerned to put it mildly.

Looking back, I now realize that parental worry was the driving force that helped to uncover one of this nation's most tragic environmental disasters. At the time, in the late 1970's, I was the environmental reporter for a small daily newspaper in Niagara Falls, New York. Though the city is a favorite destination for tourists from around the world, its economic backbone has always been the petro-chemical industry. When a problem developed in a Niagara Falls neighborhood because of the waste disposal practices of that industry, it sounded a powerful warning to the city's parents and to parents across the nation.

By now, the story of that neighborhood—commonly known as Love Canal—is well known. A World War II–era chemical dump, dormant for decades, had suddenly awakened, spilling its toxic brew into homes and schools nearby. Chemicals, many of them highly poisonous, seeped into basements and backyards. Family pets died mysteriously. Once-productive vegetable gardens suddenly wilted under the chemical onslaught.

For those families trapped in that nightmare, the concern wasn't pets or gardens, but something infinitely more precious: their children. Babies were born severely underweight; birth defects were all too common. Parents wondered if the chemical brew was responsible for their children's learning disabilities and psychological problems. Unfortunately, the Love Canal families never received straight answers to their questions for a variety of political and scientific reasons. For some of those parents, that uncertainty exists to this day.

Undoubtedly, the Love Canal disaster was an extreme case, more severe than anything most parents will ever face. Nevertheless, there are some parallel situations that threaten families today. In so many ways, parents face the same sort of uncertainty that confronted those Love Canal families nearly two decades ago. And we all share their concern for the health of our children.

Hardly a week passes without some news about a new risk: pesticides in our food; chemicals on the neighbor's lawn; asbestos in our community schools; radon gas in the family basement; leaded paint in our homes. In the Virginia community where I now live, I continue to be struck by the level of concern—and misunderstanding. How much should we worry? What is a parent to do?

It is something my wife, Joan, and I have contemplated often as we raised our two children. Fortunately, my professional background helped us steer through the minefield of risks. I sympathize with those of you who don't have the necessary information to make those crucial decisions, but remember: your concern is an important first step. As parents, we are driven by that universal worry about the safety of our children. They are so naive, so vulnerable for a variety of biological reasons I'll explain in the upcoming pages. Since they don't really know how to assess danger, they instinctively trust us, their parents, to make the right choices when it comes to their health and safety.

Obviously, one of our most important jobs as parents is to protect our children. We can't control everything about the world we live in, but it is within our power to work to protect our children's environment in our homes and neighborhoods. At first, this sounds like a pretty straightforward task, but it's complicated in the extreme by fearmongering headlines, contradictory research studies, and anecdotal reports from neighbors, relatives, and other laymen. It's as easy to overestimate the risks as it is to underestimate them.

If lead is a problem, how much of a problem is it? And is the "solution" worse than the problem itself? If you're looking to buy a house and the radon test comes up positive, should you still move ahead to the closing? Are you better off cleaning out the asbestos in your ancient furnace or letting it be? Where's the happy medium between putting your child in a biohazard suit and letting him frolic among the paint chips? We want to protect our children, but we don't want to go so overboard that we spend more time worrying than enjoying them.

I wrote this book to help you assess and prioritize your concerns about your child's safety, then give you the no-nonsense answers you need, the specific actions you can take, and some of the resources you can turn to for help.

In each and every case I've tried to provide you with the latest scientific research and opinion. I've suggested a range of options for removing or minimizing the risk, if you feel it exists, and provided ideas for where you can turn for additional advice and assessment from experts in the field. But first, a word of caution. Risk assessment—a statistical method of determining what the level of risk might be—is a scientific exercise fraught with uncertainty.

# CONTENTS

# Kidsafe

# INTRODUCTION

**A** glance at a sleeping child brings out our most tender concerns. Fast asleep in their beds, our kids seem so small, so helpless. This perception reflects reality. If children seem more vulnerable, it's because they really are.

Why is this? First, children tend to be in situations where they're likely to be exposed to some hazard. They poke around under the sink where we keep the dishwasher detergent. They contentedly wallow around in piles of sand or dirt, where they're likely to come in contact with pesticides or some other toxic chemical. They crawl around on hands and knees, exposing themselves to anything dirty or dangerous on the floor. And, with their hand-to-mouth tendencies, they are much more likely than an adult to cram something hazardous into their mouths.

Moreover, once they have been exposed to something toxic, children's physiology places them at greater risk than an adult with the same exposure. There are several reasons for this. First, children have a faster metabolism than adults—they need it to support their rapid growth—and they are much more active. These two factors mean that they're more likely to inhale larger quantities of hazardous air pollutants. Second, they absorb contaminants much more efficiently than adults because their rate of metabolism is higher. Third, their immune systems aren't fully developed, so they're more likely to be harmed by a contaminant that an adult's immune system would be able to dispatch easily. Fourth, their developing nervous system is much more vulnerable to toxic agents. Finally, because of their size, the same amount of hazardous material will affect children more severely than adults; inhaling the same toxic fumes will affect a 20-pound person much more than a 150-pound person.

The consequences of exposure to an environmental hazard can have long-lasting consequences for a child. Toxic exposures can interfere with a child's development in a variety of ways, impairing his or her ability to learn or causing behavioral problems. The damage can be temporary or permanent. Unfortunately, we have little information on how current exposures can affect a child's future health. It is known, however, that in extreme cases exposures can impair the function of vital organs or give rise to cancer later in life.

How do you cope with such dismal prospects? Obviously, you want to do your best to keep your child's environment healthy and clean. But which of these hazards are cause for real concern? To give you a little perspective, consider the following statistics, which cover people in all age brackets.

| Cause of Death | Deaths Annually in the U.S | Frequency |
|---|---|---|
| Heart Disease | 710,000 | 1 in 3 |
| Auto Accidents | 50,000 | 1 in 42 |
| Drowning | 7,500 | 1 in 280 |
| Lightning | 110 | 1 in 20,000 |

SOURCE: *National Safety Council*

In other words, in terms of absolute physical danger, riding in a car is probably riskier than almost any environmental hazard. So before you spend all your time worrying about whether or not those nearby power lines are harmful, make certain you've taken one of the most important steps toward safeguarding your child by putting him or her in a government-approved child's car seat each and every time you go anywhere in your car—no exceptions! And for children over age five, seat belts should be the rule. When you consider all the risks your child faces every day, it makes sense to put the most effort into preventing those that place him or her at greatest risk.

Let's return to those power lines for a moment. The whole issue of electromagnetic radiation from power lines and its effect on health has been a subject of great concern in the media, and that concern has certainly been taken up by parents. Research has demonstrated that the "normal" rate of childhood leukemia is 1 in 20,000. The rate of childhood leukemia for those children who have been exposed to long-term electromagnetic radiation (see chapter 3) is still pretty low: 1 in 8,000. While it's horrible to contemplate even a single case of childhood leukemia, compare that risk to the 1 in 42 odds of being injured in a car crash, and you can get some sense of perspective. Again, I must emphasize that scientists have a very hard time establishing risk—and agreeing on relative dangers—when it comes to evaluating environmental hazards, so I wouldn't consider these electromagnetic radiation figures hard and fast. But comparing odds can give you a sense of scale when you try to determine relative risk.

So what do the professionals at the Environmental Protection Agency consider the biggest threats to children's health? They rate indoor air quality (see chapter 4) the most significant threat. Other experts rank outdoor air and water pollution and electromagnetic radiation fairly high. How do you decide what are the biggest risks for your children? By following the advice in this book, you can identify the risk from most common environmental sources and minimize that risk to help keep your family healthy. But through it all, keep your perspective—and always buckle up for safety!

Often, risk assessment raises as many questions as it resolves. The same is true of epidemiology—the science of tracking disease patterns. One of the greatest shortcomings of epidemiology is its inability to detect the cause of illness among small populations. For example, if three of your neighbors have asthmatic children, epidemiologists aren't going to be able to tell you whether it's being caused by something in the air around your houses. Unfortunately, lawmakers, regulatory agencies, and parents all realize that submitting to the scientific uncertainty about assessing an individual's risk means living with a paralysis caused by inaction.

This uncertainty is especially frustrating for parents. When we ask, Is this a problem for my child? we want a "yes" or a "no"—never a "maybe." When it comes to the health of our children, we can't wait years—or decades—for an answer. What you will read in this book is, I hope, the best current assessment—and advice—about the risks facing your children. I hope you'll use this book along with your own good common sense, and I surely hope that your family is healthier as a result.

# Lead

## Your Number-One Health Risk

For years, consumers confidently used products with the blind assumption that someone—presumably a government agency and the manufacturer—had assessed those products and determined that they posed little or no risk to human health or the environment. After all, if it was widely used and readily available, it must be safe, right?

Unfortunately, history has proven otherwise. Consider the examples of asbestos, urea formalde-hyde foam, and the pesticide DDT. In each case, scientists discovered the product's potency and potential to harm only after decades of widespread use and a heavy toll on human health and the environment.

Asbestos, once thought to be a miracle insulator, has turned out to be a potent carcinogen. Litigation—much of it by workers exposed to asbestos fibers on the job—has bankrupted several major corporations and threatens to tie up the courts for years. Asbestos abatement is a multi-million dollar industry. Schools close while administrators rush to remove or contain exposed asbestos that could pose a threat to students. Meanwhile, thousands have died and countless others suffer from debilitating asbestos-related lung diseases.

Another "miracle insulator," urea formaldehyde foam, was the product of choice during the energy-conscious 1970s. Hundreds of thousands of homes were insulated with it until scientists belatedly linked the foam to a variety of illnesses.

DDT, once the farmer's miracle pesticide, was later shown to wreak havoc on wildlife and the environment. Who can forget the images of distorted animal fetuses and misshapen bird eggs?

Unfortunately, lead, a widely used metal with a history that dates to the Roman Empire, has been shown to pose the same dire threats to human health as these other products once thought so safe. (In fact, many historians believe that the widespread use of lead in Roman times—and the poisoning it caused—helped bring about the collapse of that once-omnipotent empire.) Lead is ubiquitous in our lives—it's in our plumbing, pottery, and a host of other consumer products. Until 1978, when it was banned, lead was an additive in most types of paint, so the chances are excellent that unless your house was constructed after that time, you grew up in a house whose every wall and ceiling was contaminated with lead. Until the late 1970s, lead was also added to nearly every gallon of gasoline sold in the United States—remember when you had to specify leaded or unleaded at the filling station? And that means that for decades, millions and millions of cars spewed lead-filled exhaust into the air.

In recent years, scientists have begun to understand the magnitude of the problem. With each new revelation, lead has emerged as one of the most significant threats to children's health today. In 1991, the two key federal agencies charged with protecting and safeguarding our environment—the Centers for Disease Control (CDC) and the Environmental Protection Agency (EPA)—finally acknowledged the tremendous risk. Their grim assessment: for children, lead poisoning is the nation's leading environmental health hazard. Lead poisoning, both agencies said, is "our most societally devastating disease."

## How Does Lead Harm Children?

Lead poisoning, which occurs when a person ingests lead or inhales airborne lead particles, can cause brain damage. Studies have shown that even low levels of lead poisoning can cause learning disabilities, hyperactivity, and a host of behavioral problems, including increased aggressiveness, sluggishness, confusion, and irritability. Extreme cases of lead poisoning can even cause death.

Most studies of lead poisoning conclude that it appears to lower children's IQs, although it is difficult to estimate the degree of damage and determine its permanence. It does appear that some of the damage caused by lead poisoning is irreversible despite treatment, which involves the use of chelating agents that bind to lead and remove it from the bloodstream. Sadly, newspapers abound with stories of bright, well-adjusted young children whose temperament and ability to learn seem to have been permanently compromised by severe lead poisoning. The younger the child, the more severely affected he or she will be. Given equal exposures to lead, children will absorb more lead than adults. What's worse, absorption seems to be greater in children who have an iron deficiency. Pregnant women should be aware that their developing fetuses can also be severely harmed by exposure to lead, and those women should heed the same advice offered for young children to safeguard against poisoning.

## Who Gets Lead Poisoning?

Scientists aren't precisely sure how many children are affected, but the estimates are staggering. The conservative guess is that one in every six children under the age of six has a troublesome lead level in his or her system.

But even those numbers can mislead—especially if you assume, as many people do, that lead poisoning is mostly a problem for lower-income inner-city children. Certainly that impression was fostered by the ubiquitous commercials years ago that showed disadvantaged children eating lead-filled paint chips in rundown tenement buildings. While the "pica balloon" campaign served to alert parents to the dangers of lead, it may also have failed to communicate strongly enough that this danger crosses all socioeconomic borders. In Oakland, California, for example, two of three children have excessive levels of lead in their blood. Parents should understand that every child is potentially at risk.

Many parents fail to appreciate this risk. They think to themselves, Well, if I was raised in a house filled with lead paint and I'm okay, why should I have to worry about my child? I think the more important consideration is whether *any* amount of damage from lead poisoning could impede your child's ability to reach his or her full potential. Who can ever say how much more any child could have become had he or she not been exposed to some toxic agent? We don't need the answers to be any clearer than they already are to take effective preventive action.

## What Are the Sources of Lead in the Environment?

Lead can come from a number of sources both inside and outside the home or school.

Experts estimate that as many as 75 percent of all homes built before the 1980s may contain lead paint. Although lead was banned as a paint additive in 1978, there is no guarantee that any paint bought or used after that time is harmless. After all, a store may have sold off its excess inventory of lead-filled paint after the cut-off point. And who hasn't stored leftover gallons of paint in the basement for future touch-up jobs? The point is, it's never best to assume that the paint inside or outside your home is lead-free. You should always check it for yourself; I'll explain how to do this later in the chapter.

It's not the paint sticking to your walls that poses the hazard. It's the chips of flaking paint that young children, with their famous penchant for putting anything and everything into their mouths, are likely to ingest. Even if you have no noticeable flaking, you can easily expose your children to hazardous lead dust when sanding painted woodwork or walls. In fact, lead poisoning first became a "yuppie" issue when newspapers began to chronicle the disasters that occurred when well-intentioned middle-class couples bought their dream Victorian fixer-uppers and proceeded to renovate these homes, releasing clouds of lead dust and unknowingly exposing their children to its toxic effects. But renovation isn't the only time to be careful: even the simple act of opening and closing doors and windows can unleash hazardous lead dust.

Lead paint isn't the only problem. Nearly one-third of our cities have lead somewhere in the water distribution system. The Environmental Protection Agency estimates that more than 32 million people may be exposed to unsafe levels of lead in their drinking water, a chilling thought for those parents mixing water and powdered formula for their infants.

In some communities, particularly those in inner cities or heavily industrialized areas, the levels of lead in the soil are astronomically high. Why is the problem worse in the cities? Though some of the airborne lead may have come from factories, most of the urban problem has been traced to motor vehicles. In fact, soil tests in many urban areas—especially those near busy highways—have detected elevated levels of lead, making urban dust a potential source of exposure.

Fortunately, there is some good news on this front. Recent tests show that efforts to remove lead from the environment are showing modest signs of success. Because of the government's efforts to eliminate leaded gasoline, ambient levels of lead in the air are declining rapidly. For the first time, some cities are reporting that the total number of children affected by lead poisoning is starting to decline.

Although paint, plumbing, and soil are the major threats, there are other sources of lead about which you should be aware. For example, although it is unlikely that you'll be serving drinks to your children in fine crystal, be aware that some leaded glass can pose a problem. The best advice is not to let liquids, particularly juices with high acid content such as orange or tomato juice, sit in leaded crystal glasses or containers.

Some ceramic dishes are coated with lead glazes. Imported ceramics are generally the most likely culprits. It is impossible to tell by appearance alone whether a dish contains lead; you'll have to test it. If you have any doubts, don't use ceramic dishes for your kids.

Cans of imported foods can sometimes contain lead as well. The best way to avoid the problem is to transfer foods to another container. Don't leave leftovers in the can—again, acid foods such as tomato products are the biggest offenders here; transfer them to glass or plastic containers.

Although the possibility may be remote, be aware that your pets can carry lead-filled dust and dirt in from outdoors. The best remedy is to make certain that you wash the children's hands after they pet the dog or cat.

## How Can I Tell if My Child Has Been Affected?

Don't spend a lot of time worrying. The fastest and simplest way to find the answer is to have your child tested. The Centers for Disease Control recommends that testing first be done when the child is twelve months old and again at twenty-four months. If you live in a place where you suspect the risk of lead contamination is high (for example, in an inner-city neighborhood or a home built before 1978), the CDC recommends that you first have your child screened for lead poisoning at six months of age. Ask your pediatrician to recommend how often to perform additional tests. Children older than six years should be screened at least once every two years.

Don't depend on parental instinct to decide when to have your child tested; the early symptoms of lead poisoning are so subtle that many parents won't even notice them. Again, don't waste time wondering or guessing. Ask your pediatrician for a blood lead test, which is the most accurate way to determine the concentration of lead in the blood. The test costs between fifteen and sixty dollars and requires a finger prick to collect the sample. Some communities even offer free testing, usually through the local health department. You may be entitled to free testing if you are receiving benefits under Medicaid.

A less reliable indicator is the erythrocyte protoporphyrin test. Government scientists say that this test is less expensive but often unreliable—especially at lower lead concentrations—because it doesn't directly measure lead in the blood but instead analyzes certain biochemical effects of toxic exposure.

## How Do I Interpret the Results?

Test results will usually be expressed in micrograms of lead per deciliter of blood. The Centers for

Disease Control now says that 10 or more micrograms per deciliter could represent a lead poisoning risk. This new standard was adopted after studies concluded that the old cutoff of 25 micrograms per deciliter was too high.

Several studies in the United States and abroad estimate that a child's IQ can drop ten points or more if his or her lead levels are 10 micrograms per deciliter or higher. According to these studies, the IQ levels of lead-exposed children were, on average, 5 percent lower than those of their unexposed classmates. An Australian study also found that lead exposure seemed to do the most damage when it occurred between the ages of fifteen months and four years. The CDC has reported similar results, including problems with delayed development, hyperactivity, and inattentiveness among affected children.

## What Should I Do if My Child Tests High?

If your child's blood test shows that he or she has been exposed to high levels of lead, you should take immediate action in two areas. First, consult your pediatrician about treating your child; second, identify the source of the lead problem and correct it.

## How Can I Treat Lead Poisoning?

In some cases, lead can be removed from a child's bloodstream by a process called chelation therapy. Your child will be injected once or several times with a medication that forms chemical bonds with the lead so that it can be filtered out of the bloodstream and flushed out of the body. A 1993 study in the *Journal of the American Medical Association* found that this treatment was especially effective for children with "moderate" lead levels of 25 to 55 micrograms per deciliter.

As I mentioned earlier, children who get enough iron and calcium will absorb less lead when exposed. Make certain that your child eats such iron-rich foods as lean red meat, eggs, and legumes; ask your pediatrician if your child needs an iron supplement. Rich sources of calcium include low- or nonfat milk, yogurt, and cheese, tofu coagulated with calcium, and salmon and sardine consumed with the soft bones.

## Finding—or Preventing—the Problem

Since you're aware that the two primary sources of lead in the home or school are paint and plumbing, it makes sense to focus your attention there.

## Lead Paint

If you live in an older home or apartment, there's an excellent chance that it contains some lead paint. Check the condition of wall and trim paint carefully, especially in those areas used regularly by children. If the paint is in good shape or has been covered over completely with a nonlead paint, your chance of having a problem is minimal. But if

the paint is flaking and chipping, or if you are planning to remove it yourself or hire an outside contractor to do the job, you could risk significant lead exposure.

The best advice is to test your paint yourself or have it checked by an expert. A home testing kit, available at many hardware and children's department stores as well as through many children's catalogs, usually costs about twenty dollars. The test takes about a minute; you swab a chemical solution on the painted surface in question and wait to see if the spot turns red—a sign of lead. Unfortunately, some experts say that these home-testing kits aren't always reliable.

You can also have your paint tested by an expert. Check your local health department first to see if they offer the service; many do for a nominal fee. If not, find an EPA-certified lab to do the test. They'll ask you to bring in a paint chip and will probably charge at least forty dollars for the analysis. An even costlier option would be to have a technician come to your home to do the testing.

When you're checking for lead, don't forget to check around doors and windows. Every time you open and close a door or window, the friction unleashes a small amount of paint, which may contain lead. Though this may seem like an insignificant source, over time it can produce enough contaminated dust to be a problem.

One final word of caution: don't forget the exterior of your home; it could be covered with lead paint, too. You can use the same tests on the outside of your home as you do on the inside.

If you do find lead paint, don't even think about sanding or sandblasting it off; you may end up increasing your risk of lead exposure because you'll essentially be turning the lead paint into lead dust. Your best option is either to cover the old surface with nonlead latex paint or have the old paint removed by experts trained in lead abatement.

## Checking Your Plumbing

It's a bit more difficult to anticipate whether you'll have lead in your pipes because the problem doesn't always correlate with the age of your dwelling. Older homes may have lead pipes; newer homes have copper pipe joined together with lead solder. Both can pose potential risks. Homes with soft water, which leaches more lead from pipes, are more likely to have problems than homes with hard water. And although older homes are more likely to have a problem with lead paint, newer homes are more likely to have problems with lead in the water. Even homes without lead pipes can have their drinking water contaminated by lead in the municipal water supply.

To check for problems, you could crawl around your basement inspecting pipes—which won't tell you whether the problem is in your home or with the connections between your home and the public water supply—but the easiest and most effective approach is to have your water tested. Your local water department may perform this service for free, or you may need to seek out an EPA-certified laboratory to perform the test, which usually runs less than forty dollars.

In either case, you'll probably be asked to produce two water samples for testing. The first sample is often called the "first draw"; it's the water that comes out of the pipe after the tap is first turned on. The idea here is that you want to find out how much, if any, lead leaches into your water when it's sitting around in your pipes. Ideally, your first draw sample should come from water that's been sitting overnight. Take the sample the first thing in the morning after you get up—before you've flushed the toilet or turned on the faucet to brush your teeth, wash your face, or get a drink of water. Go immediately to the tap in your kitchen and fill the container provided by the testing facility up to the line indicated.

Your second sample should be taken after you've run your faucet for a minute or two. The idea here is to see whether any lead that has leached into the water resting in the pipes is flushed out after you've kept the water running for a while. Put this "second draw" water into the second container your testing facility provided.

If your yellow pages don't yield the name of a certified lab, ask your local health department, the state environmental agency, or a regional EPA office for a list of approved testing firms. The analysis will usually take no more than a week unless the lab is unusually busy. Ask for a copy of the results in writing for your records; the report might be helpful if you ever want to sell your house and a prospective buyer questions you about lead.

Levels of 5 parts per billion or less in your water are generally considered safe. If the lead level in your water is higher than 10 parts per billion, you should consider taking remedial action.

## Other Sources of Lead

The soil in your yard could also be harboring a lead hazard. If you have an older home that's been repainted, you might want to check the soil to make certain that some inexperienced or unscrupulous painter didn't blast or sand off the old paint. A soil test is also a good idea if your home is near a major highway (remember all that leaded gasoline spewing into the air?) or has been built on or near a site

where an older—and lead-paint-contaminated—
home once stood.

As a parent, you should also be concerned about
your child's school environment. In some states,
preschools and day care centers are required to test
for lead. The same is sometimes true for public
schools, particularly the schools' water supply. Be
sure to ask your school or day care center whether
they have tested paint, water, and soil for lead and,
if so, what the results were. If the institution hasn't
performed a test, ask them to do so right away. If
they refuse, contact your local health department.

## A Word of Caution

Given the amount of public anxiety over lead exposure, you can be assured that a number of dis-
reputable companies are offering testing services.
An inaccurate analysis can hurt you either way. A
false positive—a result that tells you you've got a
lead problem when you don't—could force you
to spend money needlessly on remediation. A
false negative—a result that tells you you don't
have a lead problem when you do—could give you
an unwarranted sense of security and keep you
from making the necessary changes to eliminate
the hazard. See the resources section at the end of
this chapter for recommended testing products and
services.

## What if There's a Problem in Our Home?

### Coping with Lead Paint

Unfortunately, it's complicated to cope with lead paint in your home. If the area (or piece of furniture) causing the problem is small, you could remove the paint yourself, but only if you use a wet chemical stripper such as Peel Away or EM's Safest Stripper. Of course, these strippers themselves pose hazards for small children, so you'll need to seal off the area so that they won't inhale the fumes or run the risk of ingesting the stuff. If you use a sander or sandpaper to catch whatever paint the stripper doesn't remove, you'll also need to work in an area away from children and scrub or wet vacuum your workspace when you're through to clean up any lead paint residue. Wear a disposable respirator and ventilate the area. Don't forget that you'll probably have lead paint dust all over your clothes and hair by the time you've finished, so be careful not to track it back to clean areas.

However, if you've got a large area to decontaminate, I definitely don't recommend that you attempt to remove the paint yourself, since most removal methods will create a toxic lead dust that will only make the hazard more severe. There are latex coatings available (Encapsulastic and Certane are both recommended by experts) to seal the lead paint. You can also cover the area with tile, wallboard, carpeting, paneling, or wallpaper. If those alternatives aren't appealing—or if the paint is in such poor condition that you feel it must be removed because it would flake off even if you painted over it—you should have it removed by an expert. Ask your local health department or EPA office to recommend a reputable contractor. Be forewarned, however: removing lead paint can get costly. Removing all the lead paint from the interior of an average-sized home could easily cost $10,000. The amount spent on lead abatement is sometimes tax deductible; check with an accountant or other tax expert. If the amount of lead paint to be removed is substantial, you may need to temporarily relocate your family while the experts do their work.

### Getting the Lead Out of Your Water

If the problem is with your water pipes, the solution may be simple. Often, lead levels drop dramatically after the tap has been on for at least sixty seconds. You can double-check this by looking at the results of the first- and second-draw samples you had analyzed; the second figure is most likely much lower than the first. If the second-draw water level is under the approved lower limit for lead, you'll avoid exposure simply by running the water from the cold tap for a minute before you use it, and by always using cold water to prepare formula, juice, or food for you and your family. (Hot water leaches more lead from pipes.) You might want to time that minute the first few times you let the tap run to get a feel for how long the water is on; you may be surprised to find that it's longer than you think. If you don't like the idea of wasting that water, you can save it to clean with or use to water your plants. If you use the tap in the bathroom to fill a glass of water for drinking, remember to run that faucet for a minute before using too.

If running the tap doesn't reduce lead levels to within acceptable limits, you'll need to replace some of your plumbing—which can be a costly proposition—or switch to bottled water for drinking and cooking. Several firms offer water filters that will remove lead, although you should investigate carefully before buying, since these products have a wide range of effectiveness. The EPA certifies those filters that it deems effective; it also has a hotline that offers further advice: (800) 426-4791. The filter favored by *Consumer Reports* as of this writing is the Omni Total OT-1, which costs about one hundred dollars. However, as consumer interest in abating lead increases, new models of water lead filters are sure to emerge, so you should check all reliable sources before purchasing the most up-to-date model. I've listed some sources for filters at the end of this chapter.

### Coping with Contaminated Soil

If testing reveals that you've got a serious soil lead contamination problem, EPA inspectors may suggest that you dig out and remove up to twelve inches of topsoil from the area abutting your house to as far out as the problem extends. In particularly severe cases, this could amount to digging up your whole lawn and disposing of the soil in an approved landfill. Such cases, however, are rare. If you have a more minor problem, you can probably minimize exposure by laying peat moss or pine bark over the area in question. An EPA inspector can give you more specific information.

### Keeping the Lead Out: Simple Precautions

After you've taken steps to get the lead out of your paint, water, and soil, you might want to follow these simple precautions to further minimize your youngsters' risk of exposure. Remember, small children tend to put their fingers (or pacifiers or bottles) in their mouths regardless of where they've been.

■ Wash your children's hands regularly with warm, soapy water—especially before meal- and snacktimes, naps, or bedtime.

- Keep play areas clean and as dust-free as possible.
- Make certain that you wash pacifiers and bottles if they fall on the floor or on the ground before giving them back to your child.
- Mop floors and wipe down window ledges and any chewable surfaces (like crib bars) with a solution of one tablespoon of powdered dishwasher detergent to a gallon of warm water at least twice a week. Dishwasher detergents contain higher levels of phosphate and tend to work better than most multipurpose cleaners.
- Wash toys regularly in warm, soapy water.
- Avoid excessive dust inside your home by vacuuming frequently. A wet vacuum works best because it keeps the dust down and helps prevent it from spreading further. If you don't have a wet vacuum, mop any hard surfaces with a solution of dishwasher detergent and warm water.

## Check the Lead Before You Move

A final word about homes. If you are thinking about renting or buying a new home or apartment, be aware that Congress passed a law in 1992 requiring all landlords or homesellers to disclose the presence of lead paint in any dwelling built before 1978. Make certain you ask before you rent or buy.

# CHECKLIST

☐ Have your children tested for blood lead levels; repeat the testing as often as your pediatrician recommends.

☐ Inspect your home inside and out for lead in the paint, water supply, and soil.

☐ Take immediate measures to reduce or eliminate lead exposure. Hire EPA-certified experts when necessary.

☐ Take simple precautions to minimize your children's ingestion of lead dust—remember their hand-to-mouth existence!

## RESOURCES

### For More Information

The following experts can field a range of questions on lead poisoning prevention and will also send you fact sheets and free brochures to help you protect your children. They will also send along a list of state agencies to contact if you need advice or assistance closer to home.

Alliance to End Childhood Lead Poisoning, 600 Pennsylvania Avenue SE, Suite 100, Washington, DC 20003, (202) 543-1147.

Centers for Disease Control, Lead Poisoning Prevention Branch, 1600 Clifton Road, Atlanta, GA 30333.

EPA Safe Drinking Water Hotline: (800) 426-4791.

National Lead Information Center (run by the EPA, CDC, and the National Safety Council): (800) LEADFYI; (800) 532-3394.

## Abatement Products

You can contact these companies for information on lead abatement products:

CERTECH, 1624 Harmon Place, Suite 209, Minneapolis, MN 55403, (612) 338-1250. Makes Certane, a latex sealant.

Encapsulation Technologies, 310-12 N. Charles Street, Baltimore, MD 21201. Sells Encapsulastic, another excellent latex sealant.

## Testing Products and Services

Lead Check, Box 1210, Framingham, MA 01701. Sells Lead Check Swabs, a home paint testing kit.

Three firms have been recommended by Consumer Reports for testing lead in drinking water:

CLEAN WATER LEAD TESTING, 29 1/2 Page Avenue, Asheville, NC 28801.
(704) 251-0518. Cost: $12.

SUBURBAN WATER TESTING LABS, 4600 Kutztown Road, Temple, PA 19560.
(800) 433-6595. Cost: $35.

NATIONAL TESTING LABORATORIES, 6151 Wilson Mills Road, Cleveland, OH 44143.
(800) 458-3330. Cost: $58.

## Water Treatment Systems

*Consumer Reports* recommends the following systems for removing lead from household water:

CULLIGAN AQUACLEAR SYSTEM H-83 ($750) and SEARS KENMORE 3490 ($399) are two reverse-osmosis systems that must be installed in your plumbing system. Both are recommended effective lead removal systems.

The SEARS DISTILLER ($100) is a slow but inexpensive system for purifying small quantities of drinking water.

The NORDIC WARE 78100 ($76) removes 83 percent of the lead but is only effective for two hundred to three hundred gallons of water.

The BRITA WATER SYSTEM OB01/OB03 ($25) is a carafe filter system that sits on top of your counter. It takes twenty minutes to filter one gallon of water. Filters must be changed every thirty-five gallons; filters are sold in packs of three for $19.

## Publications

"Lead Poisoning and Your Children," a brochure available from U.S. EPA, 401 M St. SW, Washington, DC 20460

# Pesticides

**D**espite their harmful effects, dramatically described in Rachel Carson's eye-opening book *Silent Spring*, pesticides have certainly provided valuable contributions to our society. Arguably, our plentiful—and generally wholesome—food supply is a direct consequence of effective pest and disease management made possible by the use of agricultural chemicals. Chemicals have also helped us control diseases such as malaria by wiping out mosquito vectors, contributed to the elimination of damaging insect infestations (termites, for example), and eradicated yield-reducing weeds on our nation's farmland.

These valuable contributions have come at a high price. Pesticides have created a host of health and environmental problems to the point that a growing number of environmentalists advocate a society entirely free of these chemical warriors.

For your family, a pesticide-free environment is the safest course. Unfortunately, it isn't the most realistic. Even if you choose not to use chemical-based pesticides, it is nearly impossible to keep them from intruding into your environment. Fruits and vegetables you buy in the supermarket have been sprayed vigorously on the farm. If you live in a rural area, pesticide overspray can land on your property whether you like it or not. In the suburbs, neighbors hire lawn services to spray weedkillers and other noxious chemicals that inevitably stray onto your turf. In cities, exterminators spray apartment buildings for cockroaches, ants, and other pests with little concern for the philosophical leanings of the tenants. And when your home is invaded by some creeping, crawling insect in the dead of summer, it's hard not to deal with the onslaught quickly and directly by applying a household insecticide.

What's more, indiscriminate industrial disposal practices of the past have polluted our waterways with pesticide residues. For example, along the southern shore of Lake Ontario in western New York, Mirex, a potent insecticide once used primarily to control red ants, can still be found in sediment and fish flesh even though it was banned from use years ago. The reason: careless disposal by the company in upstate New York that produced the chemical. Anglers and hunters alike have been warned that much of our fish and waterfowl are tainted to the point that health authorities consider them a cancer risk in many regions of the country.

In some communities, public water supplies contain measurable levels of pesticides—even some banned from the marketplace decades ago. Sadly, a 1990 EPA report showed that the groundwater in a majority of states contained more than fifty pesticides, some of them carcinogens and many of them long banned from the marketplace. Some of the pesticides banned by the EPA are listed in the box opposite.

Unfortunately, as that EPA study showed, even banning a pesticide doesn't end the problem. DDT, for example, was banned over two decades ago but traces of it can still be found in most waterways in the United States and in the fatty tissue of the wildlife in and around those waters. And old containers of banned products still turn up in kitchen and bathroom cabinets and on basement shelves.

| Pesticide | Use |
| --- | --- |
| Aldrin | insecticide |
| Chlordane | insecticide (termites, ants) |
| Compound 1080 | rodent control |
| DDT | insecticide |
| Diazinon | insecticide |
| Dibromochloropropane (DBCP) | soil fumigant/fruits, vegetables |
| Dieldrin | insecticide |
| Dinoseb | herbicide |
| Endrin | insecticide |
| Ethylene dibromide (EDB) | insecticide |
| Heptachlor | insecticide |
| Kepone | insecticide |
| Lindane | insecticide |
| Mirex | insecticide (fire ants) |
| Silvex | herbicide |
| Strychnine | rodent control |
| 2, 4, 5-T | herbicide |
| Toxaphene | insecticide (cotton pests) |

## What Are Pesticides, Anyway?

The term *pesticide* actually refers to a whole class of chemicals designed to eradicate some particular problem. Fungicides are used to control fungi; insecticides kill insects; herbicides kill unwanted plants and weeds; rodenticides poison rodents.

There are well over one hundred thousand different chemical formulations under the broad um-
brella term *pesticide.*

In the beginning, pesticides were derived from
inorganic substances. Heavy metals such as zinc,
mercury, and arsenic were common in pesticide
formulations. But the late 1930s saw the discovery
of a new type of pesticide formulated from synthetic organic (hydrocarbon-based) chemicals.
While these chemicals ushered in a new era of agricultural productivity, scientists later learned that
such products could be even more harmful to human health and the planet's environment than their
inorganic cousins.

Pesticides come in a number of forms: granules,
powder, liquid. Some work on contact, while others
are systemic, entering a plant through its roots or an
insect or animal pest through its digestive tract. And
not all pesticides pose an equal threat. Some are
biodegradable and lose their effectiveness in a matter of days. Several companies are now marketing
naturally occurring organic pesticides, which they
claim are safer than their synthetic cousins.

## How Are Pesticides Regulated?

The chief regulator of pesticides in our country is
the U.S. Environmental Protection Agency under

the legal authority of the Federal Insecticide, Fungicide, and Rodenticide Act (FIFRA), first passed in 1972. The agency registers all pesticides, a process that is theoretically based on an exhaustive scientific review to assess the risk to human health and the environment. Unfortunately, the system has flaws.

Among other things, the agency can decide to register a particularly troublesome pesticide if it determines that the benefits to society outweigh the potential risks, which means that chemicals that would ordinarily be banned are allowed to remain on the market. In some cases, these determinations have been made after farmers have complained that no effective substitute was available. Other chemicals—like chlordane, a potent termite poison—have been left on the market for a time, with the EPA attempting to minimize the risk by allowing sales only to qualified applicators.

Concerned that earlier methods of approval may have overlooked some particularly troublesome chemicals—or were based on outdated science—Congress in 1988 ordered the EPA to reassess the safety of all pesticides now on the market. But the review process is cumbersome, and the EPA has said it could be the end of the decade before the task is complete.

There are two other important flaws in the pesticide registration system that have serious implications for the health of you and your children:

- Nearly all the toxicity research is done by the manufacturers, and only then reviewed by the EPA.
- Universally, the estimates of risk are based on research involving laboratory animals. Scientists can then extrapolate the probable risk to *adults*—never to children. (Children will readily absorb more than adults exposed to the same amount of pesticide.)

As you can imagine, this risk assessment is not exactly a precise science. In more than one case, different scientists have looked at the same reports and reached markedly different opinions about the toxicity of a substance.

## Pesticides in Your Food

When it comes to pesticide residues and food, the issue of regulation is a little more complex. Though the EPA is also responsible for establishing maximum limits for the amount (and kind) of pesticide residue on fresh or canned fruits and vegetables, the actual enforcement of that standard is the domain of another federal agency—the Food and Drug Administration.

When our government says that the food supply is safe, they are basing that claim on tests of less than 1 percent of all fruits and vegetables, including imports. Imported produce can be particularly troublesome because some pesticides banned in the United States are still used in foreign countries and end up on imported produce available in U.S. stores.

Moreover, while a section of the Food, Drug, and Cosmetic Act called the Delaney Clause prohibits any residues of cancer-causing pesticides in foods after processing, this standard isn't always met. Unfortunately, in 1988 the EPA interpreted the law to mean "negligible risk," which means that some cancer-causing residues may be present but at levels deemed acceptable by the agency. The interpretation has been challenged in court.

The agency has also come under fire for the so-called Delaney Paradox: many carcinogenic pesticides registered before 1978 are still on the market because the EPA's review process has been so slow. This delay has tainted the reassurance of food safety from government regulators.

In 1989, the Natural Resources Defense Council challenged the EPA's claims of safety with a report called "Intolerable Risk: Pesticides in Our Children's Food." The report estimated that as many as six thousand of the nation's 22 million preschoolers would get cancer at some point in their lives because of lifetime pesticide exposure.

As a direct result of that study—and a subsequent segment on CBS's influential *60 Minutes* program—a widely used chemical called Alar was eventually removed from the market. Alar had been applied to apples and other fruit to help provide a more uniform color, presumably to enhance consumer appeal. But it was also a carcinogen that the EPA once characterized as a "potent" risk to children. Even though more recent studies for the manufacturer challenged the EPA's original concerns, public pressure forced the company to pull Alar from the market.

Part of the reason children are so vulnerable to chemicals such as Alar is that they tend to eat more vegetables, fruits, and fruit-based products such as applesauce and juice than adults. What's more, the EPA establishes its safety standards based on studies with adults, raising the possibility that children are overexposed simply because the agency hasn't adequately considered the dosage effect on smaller human beings. And for adults and children alike, the EPA's assessment for some chemicals is further outdated because of changes in the nation's dietary habits. For example, one has to question the accuracy of some EPA guidelines for fruit that are based on the assumption that the average person eats no more than one-half of a melon each year. The guidelines also are not realistic in light of recommendations from the government, as well as from the American Cancer Society and other leading health-promoting institutions, that children (and adults) should consume at least five servings of fruits or vegetables each day. In addition, guidelines like this were written decades ago; today, most fruits and vegetables are available in supermarkets year round. This fact certainly raises questions about the accuracy of the EPA's figures for annual exposure to pesticides.

## What Is the Consequence of Pesticide Exposure?

Unlike the impact of, say, eating spoiled food, where stomach upset is sure to follow in a few hours' time, the consequences of pesticide exposure may not become evident for years. Some pesticides may be carcinogenic (causing cancer), while others may be neurotoxic (damaging to the nervous system) or mutagenic (causing genetic mutations). For pregnant women, added risk can come from pesticides that are teratogenic (causing birth defects).

As noted earlier, children tend to be more vulnerable than adults to these pesticide effects, in part because their body's defense mechanisms are not fully mature. For example, the liver in a young body is not fully developed, which reduces its ability to filter toxic substances out of the bloodstream. Infants also seem more vulnerable to chemicals that affect the nervous system.

In extreme cases, pesticides have caused some children to contract multiple chemical sensitivity (MCS), a condition caused by chemical overexposure. Symptoms include irritability, fatigue, head-aches, and upper-respiratory problems. In some instances these symptoms are so severe that parents are forced to undertake the Herculean task of creating a chemical-free environment for their child.

## As a Parent, What Can I Do?

Fortunately, plenty. By taking some reasonably simple steps, you can significantly reduce the risk to your family.

*Examples of labels certifying produce is organic.*

■ The safest course would be to grow your own chemical-free produce. But as a practical matter, most families are not in a position to grow vast quantities of vegetables and fruits. The next logical step would be to buy organically grown produce in season from a farmers' market. How do you tell if produce is truly organic? A number of states, including California, Colorado, Iowa, Kansas, Maine, Minnesota, Montana, Nebraska, New Hampshire, New Mexico, North Dakota, Oregon, Texas, Vermont, Washington, and Wisconsin, have laws specifying when produce can be labeled "organic." In states with no such laws, look for a label certifying that the product meets standards set by one of the organic growers' associations, such as the Organic Crop Improvement Association, Farm Verified Organic, California Certified Organic Farmers, and Organic Growers and Buyers Association.

■ Buy only produce that is in season. Out-of-season produce is often imported and may come from a country that allows pesticides now banned in the United States.

■ Purchase your fruits and vegetables from a supermarket that conducts its own pesticide testing or specifies when produce is organically grown. The Fresh Fields supermarket chain has based its reputation, in part, on its offerings of organic produce. Other stores that test for pesticides or offer organic produce usually advertise the fact. If you have any questions, ask the produce manager.

■ When buying produce, remember that perfect-looking fruits and vegetables may be that way because the grower used lots of pesticides or waxes. Sometimes it doesn't hurt to select produce that has a few blemishes.

■ Another alternative would be to avoid fruits or vegetables that historically have high levels of pesticides, such as apples, pears, cherries, strawberries, plums, broccoli, squash, cucumbers, and most foods grown in the soil (potatoes, carrots, beets). Leafy vegetables such as lettuce and spinach also tend to have higher pesticide levels, mostly because they have more exposed surface area. Bananas, avocados, watermelons, grapefruit, oranges, pineapple, corn, cabbage, asparagus, green beans, and cauliflower tend to have lower pesticide concentrations.

■ Be somewhat suspicious of waxed fruits and vegetables. Though the wax provides a nice shiny appearance, it is sometimes treated with a fungicide to retard spoilage. You can gently scrape the skin with your fingernail to see if wax has been applied.

Regardless of where you get your produce, you can take steps during preparation to reduce risk of pesticide exposure. If you do buy waxed fruits or vegetables, peeling will help. If your produce isn't waxed, scrub it with a vegetable brush and warm, soapy water. Some manufacturers make produce rinses expressly for this purpose.

## Final Words About Pesticides and Food

- Over the past few years, several baby food makers have virtually eliminated pesticide residues, so canned baby fruits and vegetables from the supermarket may actually be healthier than similar homemade offerings. Check the label to make certain the contents were organically grown.
- All pregnant or nursing women and all children under fifteen should avoid eating fish (and even some waterfowl) from most of the nation's inland waterways, including the Great Lakes. Decades of air pollution, improper chemical disposal, and agricultural runoff have taken a toll on the nation's freshwater ecosystems. EPA tests of fish flesh have turned up dangerous levels of chemicals like dioxin, PCBs (polychlorinated biphenyls), mercury, and even DDT, which was banned

over twenty years ago but stubbornly survives in bottom sediment.

Many of these chemicals are carcinogens and most tend to accumulate in the human body. If for some reason you would prefer not to eliminate freshwater fish from your family's diet, consult your local health department for information on specific waterways and fish species. Nearly every state has advisories about freshwater fish consumption. Health authorities can also tell you how to prepare the fish to further reduce your risk.

This contamination problem does not apply to commercially available seafood in supermarkets or restaurants, where supplies are monitored for pesticides by government inspectors. Nor does it apply to products from most fish farms, where growers can carefully control water quality and eliminate other possible sources of pollution.

■ Be aware that pesticides tend to accumulate in animals' organs, so liver, kidney, and sweetbreads are more likely to be higher in pesticides than other cuts of meat.

■ There is some disagreement over the extent of pesticide risk. A Grocery Manufacturers of America study in 1992 concluded that 99 percent of all produce was free of health-threatening chemicals. The study also said the nation's food supply was one of the safest in the world. Despite these findings, many experts still recommend caution because even low levels of a pesticide can accumulate in the body over time.

## What About the Yard?

In the springtime, lawn and garden centers are filled with homeowners in search of products to help them create that perfect yard. Unfortunately, that quest often involves pesticides. Even for trained experts, applying chemicals is a tricky proposition. In the hands of an amateur, that risk can be multiplied.

Regardless of the skill of the pesticide user, chemicals and children—especially young children—do not mix. Children love to roll in the grass, run through the bushes, and climb the trees. They don't hesitate to put something in their mouths, no matter how much pesticide residue it might contain. As you contemplate that perfect lawn, consider the following:

■ More than half of all pesticide poisoning cases involve children.

- After medicine, pesticides are the most common cause of poisoning among children.
- At least one study has found elevated leukemia rates among children whose parents used pesticides in the yard or garden at least once each month.
- Children absorb pesticides through ingestion, inhalation, and skin contact. Just breathing pesticide fumes can be harmful to them.

## How Are Lawn and Garden Pesticides Regulated?

The EPA requires labels on all pesticides to denote their toxicity. "Danger" means highly poisonous; ingesting a tiny quantity could be fatal. "Warning" means moderately hazardous but still dangerous enough that one teaspoon could kill an adult. "Caution" is the least hazardous designation, meaning that fatal doses would require anything from one ounce to one pint.

Even with this labeling policy, our nation's regulatory system offers scant protection when it comes to pesticides, especially those used on lawns and gardens. Common chemicals such as diazinon, for example, are still approved for lawn use even though the EPA has decided that the product is too toxic to wildlife to be used on golf courses.

## How Can I Protect My Children?

The best course is to reduce or eliminate the use of chemicals in your yard. Resign yourself to a few weeds for the sake of your children's health.

You can consider natural alternatives to pest control. Weeds can be picked by hand. Predators such as birds, ladybugs, bats, and praying mantises help control pests. You can set up a birdhouse to attract birds. You can order ladybugs through the mail to dine on your garden pests. Plants such as marigold, onion, chives, and spearmint tend to repel undesirable insects. Strategically placed plants will help control garden infestations. A good organic gardening book will point you to more specific information.

If you use fertilizer, make sure it is organic. A number of companies now market lines of organic lawn care products. Regardless of the type, make sure you closely follow label directions for mixing and application. Wear protective clothing and gloves and always keep children and pets away from the area being sprayed. Apply only as directed: Applying twice as much as recommended does not double the chemical's effectiveness. Find out from the manufacturer how long you should keep the children away from the sprayed area. As always, make sure your children's hands are washed thoroughly after they play near the treated area.

Store all lawn and gardening products up high, out of reach of children; better yet, store them in a locked cabinet. Call your local health department to find out when and how to dispose of leftover chemicals.

And, if you must use a lawn service, ask for organic products. Most major companies, including Chemlawn, offer safer organic alternatives to chemical treatments.

## What About Inside the Home?

Avoiding pesticides inside isn't easy if your home has been infested by some creeping, crawling, or flying pest. But there are steps you can (and should) take if your children are young.

Take away the food supply of insects and rodents by carefully sweeping up crumbs, wiping spills immediately, and storing trash in tightly covered containers. Remove the animals' water supply by repairing all leaking and dripping faucets. If you still have a problem, consider either a trap or other mechanical method of control or use homemade potions concocted from natural ingredients.

For rats or mice, don't use poisons. You have three alternate choices: get a cat, use a trap, or mix up a batch of homemade poison—one that isn't a big risk to your children.

Such a natural poison can be made from one part plaster of paris and one part flour, with a little sugar and powdered cocoa mixed in (one-half teaspoon of sugar and cocoa to each tablespoon of plaster of paris and flour). If you have a major problem, call an exterminator and specify a low-toxicity spray.

For insects, consider means other than chemical sprays, which are dangerous to children and should never be used in the kitchen, where food is prepared and stored. Instead, try these alternatives. For cockroaches, soak a rag in beer and place it in a shallow dish near an infested area. In the morning, take the drunken roaches outside and dispose of them. Wipe up ants with a wet rag or sponge. Other ants won't follow because they can't locate the trail. Ants can also be discouraged by sprinkling red chili pepper or borax near where they are getting in.

Most flea sprays contain chemicals that could be toxic to your family or your pets. Powdered products can be inhaled and flea collars emit a chemical cloud around your pet that could be inhaled by your children.

As an alternative, most animal experts insist that a healthy pet doesn't usually harbor fleas. So be conscious of your pet's diet and overall living environment; it may help keep the problem to a minimum. Your pet can also be made flea resistant by mixing brewer's yeast in its food. Add about 25 milligrams per 10 pounds of food throughout the flea season. The yeast creates a skin odor unpleasant to the fleas.

Another natural repellent is citrus oil. Cut up four lemons and cover them with water in a saucepan. Bring to a boil, then simmer for about forty-five minutes. Strain the liquid and store it in a glass jar. As you brush your pet, apply the liquid liberally to the fur so that it reaches the animal's skin. Dry with towels and brush again.

You should also vacuum frequently. And, though it sounds somewhat impractical, some naturalists say the best way to remove fleas is to remove your family, pets, and houseplants from your home, close the doors and windows, and crank up the thermostat to 110 degrees or so for several hours. Most fleas cannot survive in that heat.

For mosquitoes, there are a number of natural repellents available to you and your children. Use cotton balls to wipe vinegar on exposed skin. When it dries, the odor disappears and it becomes an effective repellent. You might also buy some oil of citronella at a natural food store and dilute it with baby oil or vegetable oil (a few drops of citronella per ounce of oil) then wipe it on exposed skin. Do not use undiluted citronella because it could cause a rash.

If all else fails and you must resort to chemicals,

follow directions very carefully and keep your children away from the sprayed area.

## CHECKLIST

☐ Call your local health department to find out if your area is being sprayed with pesticides such as rodenticides to control rats and mice in public parks or aerosols to control specific insect infestations. Determine spraying schedules and try to keep your children out of those areas for as long as possible after spraying to minimize their exposure.

☐ Buy or purchase certified organic produce whenever possible, or purchase produce from supermarkets that conduct their own pesticide testing.

☐ Buy produce in season when possible.

☐ Peel produce, or scrub it with a vegetable brush and warm, soapy water before eating.

☐ Buy certified organic baby food when possible.

☐ Avoid fish and waterfowl that don't pass EPA muster.

☐ Use only organic fertilizer for your lawn; opt for natural alternatives rather than chemical sprays.

❑ Keep all pesticides out of children's reach; use them only in well-ventilated areas away from children.

❑ Use natural insect and rodent remedies inside your home.

## RESOURCES

### For More Information

Americans for Safe Food, Center for Science in the Public Interest, 1875 Connecticut Avenue NW, Suite 300, Washington, DC 20009, (202) 332-9110.

Grocery Manufacturers of America, 1010 Wisconsin Avenue NW, Suite 800, Washington, DC 20007, (202) 337-9400.

National Coalition Against the Misuse of Pesticides, 701 E Street SE, Washington, DC 20003, (202) 543-5450.

Natural Resources Defense Council, 40 W. Twentieth Street, New York, NY 10011, (212) 727-2700.

### Publications

*Diet for a Poisoned Planet* by David Steinman, Ballantine Books, 1992.

*Rodale's Chemical-Free Yard and Garden* by Fern M.
Bradley, Rodale Press, 1991.


## Organic Pesticide Suppliers

Ringer, 9959 Valley View Road, Eden Prairie, MN
55344, (800) 654-1047.

# Electromagnetic Fields

**E**pidemiologists are the detectives of the medical profession. Indeed, they often work to solve medical mysteries much the same way Peter Falk routinely solves cases as TV's rumpled Detective Columbo. Though they generally do their work with a lot less fanfare than Columbo, their detective skills are every bit as formidable.

Take Dr. Nancy Wertheimer, for example. In 1976, Wertheimer, an epidemiologist with the Colorado Health Department, began a study of childhood leukemia in Denver. With little other than anecdotal evidence to go on, she began looking at the files of 344 children who had died of cancer. Was there a common link? Had all of these children been exposed to some mysterious carcinogen?

Frustrated after a number of dead ends, Wertheimer decided to check the neighborhoods of all 344 children to see if she could uncover a clue.

As she drove around the streets of Denver, Wertheimer noticed that a number of the 344 homes were in close proximity to pole-mounted electrical transformers. It seemed to be the only common link that might explain the unusually high numbers of leukemia cases. After consulting with a physicist friend, Wertheimer decided to focus on electromagnetic radiation as a possible explanation. When she published her study in 1979, it offered compelling evidence of a link between the childhood leukemias and the low-frequency radiation emitted by nearby electrical equipment.

Though the study was initially met with a mixture of criticism and disbelief, Wertheimer's research launched a debate over the risks facing children exposed to electromagnetic fields (EMFs). Though there have been many attempts to discredit her work, the initial study has been replicated, adding further credibility to her claims of risk.

Despite such mounting evidence, the link between EMFs and cancer is still controversial. Be aware that because large-scale tests haven't been conducted, some scientists still aren't convinced that a serious threat exists. But they are being strongly challenged by those experts who are convinced that there is a correlation between EMF exposure and childhood cancer, and who point to a growing body of evidence that validates their beliefs:

- In a 1975 study, Dr. Robert Becker, head of orthopedic surgery at the Veterans Administration hospital in Syracuse, New York, had suggested that electromagnetic fields might promote the growth of cancerous cells.
- A 1982 study by Washington State researcher Samuel Milham reported twice the expected rate of leukemia among utility workers.
- In a landmark 1985 court case, H. Dickson Montague, a lawyer for the Klein Independent School District in Houston, used an array of medical experts to successfully argue that the local utility company should pay damages and remove a 345,000-volt power line installed too close to an elementary school.
- A follow-up study in 1987 by North Carolina epidemiologist David Savitz verified the Wertheimer findings. The results stunned many in the scientific community because it was assumed that Savitz, who conducted the study for the utility industry, would refute the earlier findings.
- A 1989 study by Congress's Office of Technology Assessment concluded that evidence

indicated there was some degree of risk associated with electromagnetic radiation exposure. However, the study also pointed out that the evidence was inconclusive and said that more research was needed before any decision could be made regarding the need for federal regulation.

- A 1990 Environmental Protection Agency report said that the evidence of risk was too strong to be a coincidence but was not overwhelming enough to erase all scientific doubt about the link between electromagnetic radiation and cancer.
- In a 1991 study for the electric utility industry, University of California scientist John Peters concluded that exposure to strong magnetic fields could increase the risk of childhood leukemia up to two and a half times. Dr. Peters also said that exposure to some household appliances could double the risk of cancer.

## What Is an Electromagnetic Field?

Any time electricity passes through wires, power lines, or appliances (when they are on), it creates an electromagnetic field. That field consists of low-level radiation produced by the oscillating electrical current. Though scientists don't fully understand the phenomenon, they suspect that this radiation can disrupt certain biological processes. According to some medical theories, this disruption could promote the growth of cancerous cells.

In today's electricity-dependent society, EMFs surround us. Outside, huge power grids and transformers carry hundreds of thousands of volts of electricity from the power plant to our homes. Inside, homes are loaded with EMF sources: microwave ovens, computers, fluorescent lights, televisions, hair dryers, electric razors, electric blankets, clock radios, and dozens of other common household appliances. In short, nearly everything that operates on electricity is a potential EMF source.

Electromagnetic fields are measured in units called milligauss (mG). Some experts feel that a field stronger than 2.5 mG is cause for concern. Later in the chapter, I'll discuss how you can measure the EMF fields in and around your home.

## Who Regulates This Radiation?

At this point there is no federal standard limiting the amount of radiation from power lines or appliances. Several states have attempted to fill the void by setting standards for new power line construction. A 1989 report by the congressional Office of Technology Assessment cited scientific uncertainty when it recommended against setting federal standards. At the same time, the National Institute for Occupational Safety and Health has suggested there may be a need for workplace standards to lower EMF exposure for high-risk workers in the communications and electric utility industries.

## What About the Courts?

Though regulators have been slow to respond to concerns about EMFs, the courts haven't been as timid. In addition to the Houston school case, a number of major lawsuits have been won (or settled) following claims of EMF exposure. In addition, landowners in several states have successfully sued over power line easements with the claim that EMFs had severely devalued the worth of their property.

## What Should a Parent Do?

Though the scientific jury is still out, most experts would recommend that parents follow a prudent course by taking steps to reduce EMF exposure. But this conservative course is not just for children: pregnant women should be just as cautious because of possible risk to the fetus.

In most cases, homes with high EMF fields lie close to high voltage power lines, so you should minimize outside exposure by keeping children away from the area. But you can also take steps to reduce your child's exposure inside your home. As a parent, you should remember this basic rule: the greater the distance from the source, the lower the EMF exposure will be.

Homes should be a minimum of 400 feet from a long-distance, high-voltage power line and at least 150 feet from local high-current lines (not including the line into your house). If you feel your home is too close (or is near some other electrical installation such as a substation) call your local utility company and ask them to test your home. Needless to say, you should carefully check new neighborhoods for nearby power lines if you are contemplating a move.

You can hire a professional testing firm to measure EMF levels in your home or neighborhood. The cost will be around three hundred dollars and should include a written report of the findings. But perhaps the best way to evaluate your environment is to buy or rent a gaussmeter. It will cost less than professional testing and will allow you to check your entire home thoroughly. Renting a gaussmeter will run about $60 a week; operating the device is relatively straightforward. Purchasing a good meter will cost at least $275, though some models can be purchased for about $100 (see the resources section at the end of the chapter). You could always share the cost with other families who have an interest in testing their homes.

How will you interpret the reading? The fields in most homes range from 0.5 to 10.0 mG. A study of Denver homes found that 90 percent were in the 1.82 mG range.

Outdoor readings (a concern for playgrounds and yards) should probably not exceed 2.0–2.5 mG. Though government agencies are just beginning to grasp the extent of the problem, several states have established limits for EMFs near power lines. Among the states with limits are Florida, Minnesota, Montana, New Jersey, New York, North Dakota, and Oregon. If you live in one of those states, consult the appropriate agency for further advice.

Be aware that there are many potential sources of EMFs outdoors. In San Francisco, for example, high readings have been found on streets where electric buses run. Similar problems have been found near subways and electric Amtrak train lines. Some apartment buildings, factories, and office buildings have transformers on the premises to step up or step down current. These transformers can be a source of high EMF readings.

## What Should I Do If EMFs Are High Outdoors?

What if there is a problem? If EMF readings are elevated in a public place like a school, park, or playground, notify the local health authorities.

If the readings are high around an apartment building or in a residential neighborhood, tell your neighbors first, then contact the appropriate authority (your landlord, the local utility company, etc.) and ask that action be taken. If a utility has proposed new services in (or through) your neighborhood, make sure the installation provides an adequate space buffer between homes and electrical lines. A number of homeowners' groups nationwide have either blocked new construction or forced utilities to reroute new power lines away from residential areas.

## What Should I Do About EMFs Inside My Home?

Ultimately, the best way to protect your family is to thoroughly test your home with a gaussmeter. As mentioned earlier, the average reading for most homes will be between 0.5 and 10.0 mG.

To conduct a thorough survey, first draw a free-hand plan of your home, then make a list of rooms so you can record each reading. You should also make a list of appliances to test. The best time to test your home is during peak usage so you'll know you've gotten the highest possible readings.

Starting outdoors, take readings at the four corners of the house about three feet from the ground and three feet from the wall. Next, find the place where the electrical lines enter your home. Take a reading there, then measure again six feet to either side of the entry point. Mark each of the test points on your sketch and record the results.

Start your indoor measurements at the front door. Then find the point along the wall where the service enters the house and measure there.

Next, test the most frequently used rooms. Take the measurements in the center of the room, three feet from the floor. If the room contains a number of electrical devices (such as a family room with a TV, VCR, stereo, and some video games), take a reading in the spot where most of your family would sit while in that room. In bedrooms, measure about a foot above the center of the bed. Check areas around clocks, radios, and other appliances. If you have electric heat, test near the heating units. Check the bathroom and kitchen with all the usual appliances turned on.

After you've tested all except seldom-used rooms, look at the individual readings for each room. Average all the indoor numbers.

If readings seem at or near normal, relax. If they are elevated (or are elevated only in certain places), see if a simple adjustment will suffice. If readings are high near a favorite chair, can it be moved? If a baseboard heating element is causing high readings near a child's bed, can the bed be moved farther away?

What if the cause of the problem isn't obvious? Find the main electrical panel in your house and shut off the main power switch. Take readings again. If they are still high, then chances are that the source is outside your home. You may want to call your utility company and ask them to come and test the power lines near your house.

If the high readings disappear when the main power switch is off, the problem is most likely inside your home, and you may want to consult a professional EMF tester to find the source. Sometimes, unusual wiring configurations are responsible (for example, a ground wire could be transferring electricity to metal plumbing pipes). Professionals can track down the problem quickly, and an electrician should be able to correct the problem by installing the correct wiring.

## How Can I Use Appliances Safely?

Electrical appliances are one of the major sources of strong EMFs in the home. Keep your children away from appliances that emit a strong field, including electric blankets, water beds with electric heaters, dishwashers, and microwave ovens (two out of three children between the ages of four and twelve use microwaves). The same advice is true for pregnant women. Instead of standing in front of the operating appliance, move away or into the next room.

For appliances with lower fields, advise children to keep their distance: at least three feet from a television or video game; at least two feet from a computer screen (EMFs are as high as 28 mG at four inches; 1 mG at twenty-eight inches). Keep all electrical devices (clocks, radios, etc.) at least thirty inches from a child's bedside, or use battery-powered or wind-up versions, which don't emit EMFs. And though children aren't likely to be heavy users of cellular phones, several studies have suggested a possible link to brain cancer, so caution may be in order.

To help guide you, here is a general list of appliances and their approximate EMF readings at different distances.

| Appliance | Field at Four Inches (mG) | Field at Three Feet (mG) |
| --- | --- | --- |
| Blender | 50–220 | 0.3–1.1 |
| Can opener | 1,300–4,000 | 0.5–7.0 |
| Clothes dryer | 4.8–110 | 0.1–1 |
| Coffee maker | 6–29 | <0.1 |
| Computer | 10–28 | <1.0 |
| Electric drill | 350–500 | 0.8–2.0 |
| Electric razor | 14–1,600 | <0.1–3.3 |
| Fluorescent light | 40–123 | <0.1–2.8 |
| Hair dryer | 3–1,400 | <0.1–2.8 |
| Iron | 12–45 | 0.1–0.2 |
| Television | 4.8–100 | <0.1–1.5 |
| Toaster | 10–60 | <0.1 |
| Vacuum cleaner | 230–1,300 | 1.2–18 |

A word of caution: use this list only as a general guide. More and more appliance makers are taking steps to reduce EMF levels. Sunbeam, for example, has found a way to produce an electric blanket with reduced EMFs. And newer computers emit much lower levels than older models. And remember this: the degree of risk is a function of the amount of EMF emitted and the duration of exposure. Thus long-duration exposure to a weak source such as an alarm clock may be more dangerous than short-term exposure to a stronger source such as a hair dryer.

## C H E C K L I S T

☐ Locate potential sources of EMFs outside your home, including power grids, power lines, high-current lines, and transformers. If your home lies too close to these sources, contact your local utility.

☐ Check an area's EMF sources before you move into a new neighborhood.

☐ Locate potential sources of EMFs inside your home, including microwave ovens, computers, fluorescent lights, and televisions.

☐ Buy or rent a gaussmeter to measure EMF levels inside and outside your home.

☐ Teach your children to keep an appropriate distance from EMF sources, particularly computer screens and televisions.

☐ Older appliances are likely to produce stronger EMFs; consider buying newer models when possible.

## RESOURCES

### For More Information

Electric Power Research Institute, 3412 Hillview Avenue, Palo Alto, CA 94303. EPRI is an industry-supported group involved in extensive EMF research.

U.S. Environmental Protection Agency EMF Group, Office of Radiation Programs, 401 M Street SW, Washington, DC 20460.

### Testing Equipment and Services

Electric Field Measurement Company, Box 326, West Stockbridge, MA 01266, (413) 357-5124. Another gaussmeter source.

Healthful Hardware, Box 3217, Prescott, AZ 86302, (602) 445-8825. Sells gaussmeters, computer shields, and a host of other EMF-related products.

Integrity Electronics and Research, 558 Breckenridge Street, Buffalo, NY 14222. Sells a reliable gaussmeter for under $200.

Magnetic Sciences International, Box 489, 2425B Channing Way, Berkeley, CA 94704, (510) 208-5080. Also sells a low-cost gaussmeter.

SafeEnvironments, 400 Preda Street, San Francisco, CA 94577, (415) 549-9693. Does home electromagnetic testing.

## Publications

*WARNING: The Electricity Around You May Be Hazardous to Your Health* by Ellen Sugarman, Simon & Schuster, 1992.

# FOUR

# Air Pollution

During the Persian Gulf War, Iraqi soldiers ignited hundreds of wells in the oilfields of Kuwait, creating a smoky inferno that was visible for hundreds of miles. The smoke was so thick in some parts of Kuwait that day and night were virtually indistinguishable. Though the smoke created some temporary health problems, clear skies returned to Kuwait as soon as a hard-working group of Texas oil field experts extinguished the blazing wells.

Unfortunately, most of our air quality problems are not quite as obvious—nor are they as easily solved. Indeed, though the key weapon in the battle against pollution, the federal Clean Air Act, is now more than two decades old, in many ways we haven't made much progress at all. The primary reason is that the problem of unhealthy air is more complex than anyone ever dreamed, extending even to the air we breathe in our homes and public buildings. To better understand the complexities of this issue—and the reason you should be concerned as a parent—let's go back to the beginning.

## Outdoor Air

One of the first mandates of the new U.S. Environmental Protection Agency created in the early 1970s was to attack urban air pollution. Many of the nation's cities were being choked by a smelly industrial haze that was being exacerbated by the uncontrolled tailpipe effluent from millions of cars and trucks. Consequently, the EPA's initial effort, the Clean Air Act of 1970, targeted both factory and motor vehicle sources by identifying seven major pollutants for regulation:

1. **Hydrocarbons:** Hydrocarbons comprise a large group of organic compounds that help form smog. Cars are the major source, but are not the only culprit; gas stations and industrial solvents are also contribu-

tors. Many hydrocarbons, including benzene, are potent carcinogens.

2. **Ozone:** This ground-level pollutant is formed by a complex chemical reaction between sunlight, hydrocarbons, and other organic compounds. Though motor vehicles are the largest single source, there are other contributors, including dry cleaners and other industries.

   Although beneficial in the earth's upper atmosphere, ozone can cause a host of respiratory problems, particularly among children and the elderly, when it's present at ground level. Nationwide, more than 75 million people are exposed to unhealthy ozone smog sometime during the year.

3. **Sulfur dioxide:** This compound is an inorganic chemical that is a byproduct of the burning of fossil fuel. Sulfur dioxide has been found to be one of the main causes of acid rain. It can cause respiratory problems in humans.

4. **Nitrogen dioxide:** Another inorganic byproduct of fossil fuel combustion that can cause respiratory problems.

5. **Carbon monoxide:** Carbon monoxide is a colorless, odorless poison gas that is produced by combustion. Sources include kerosene heaters, furnaces, water heaters, wood stoves, and automobile engines.

Even at low doses it can produce fatigue among children. In high doses it is fatal.

6. **Particulates:** Tiny particles of airborne dust and soot can cause respiratory problems. Of the six pollutants targeted initially by the EPA, particulates may have been the largest cause of the visible pollution that once hovered over many of the nation's industrialized cities.

7. **Lead:** Though the EPA's efforts to remove lead from the environment began with the first Clean Air Act, it wasn't until more than a decade later that experts realized the magnitude of the risk facing children as a result of lead emissions (see chapter 1). Though lead was emitted by a variety of industrial sources, perhaps the lion's share of the problem came from gasoline-burning motor vehicles. The EPA took the first steps toward eliminating leaded fuel in the mid-1970s when it mandated unleaded gasoline for new cars.

Even though the EPA has been working for over two decades to bring these seven pollutants under control, they have had mixed success. Particulate levels have dropped dramatically, and airborne lead has been reduced. While nitrogen dioxide levels have improved, scientists in the 1980s realized that sulfur dioxide was creating an acid rain problem, and Congress recently mandated steps to further reduce this pollutant. In addition, the EPA has not succeeded in cleaning up the air in the nation's large urban areas. Even now, a number of urban areas have unhealthy ground levels of ozone (smog).

## Metropolitan Areas with the Most Severe Air Pollution

The EPA has declared that ninety-eight areas within the United States have unhealthy levels of smog for at least part of the year. The following nine areas are rated as having the most severe problems, according to EPA testing over the past decade:

1. Los Angeles–Anaheim–Riverside, California
2. Baltimore, Maryland
3. Chicago, Illinois (and nearby Indiana and Wisconsin counties)
4. Houston-Galveston-Brazoria, Texas
5. Milwaukee-Racine, Wisconsin
6. Muskegon, Michigan
7. New York, New York (and nearby Connecticut and New Jersey counties)

8. Philadelphia, Pennsylvania (and nearby
   New Jersey and Delaware counties)
9. San Diego, California

Several other metropolitan areas are considered
to have "serious" air quality problems, though not
quite as severe as the top nine. Among the areas:

1. Atlanta, Georgia
2. Bakersfield, California
3. Baton Rouge, Louisiana
4. Beaumont–Port Arthur, Texas
5. Boston, Massachusetts
6. El Paso, Texas
7. Fresno, California
8. Hartford, Connecticut
9. Huntington, West Virginia–Ashland, Kentucky (and nearby Ohio counties)
10. Parkersburg, West Virginia–Marietta, Ohio
11. Rochester, Maine–Portsmouth and Dover,
    New Hampshire
12. Providence, Rhode Island
13. Sacramento, California
14. Sheboygan, Wisconsin
15. Springfield, Massachusetts
16. Washington, D.C. (and neighboring Mary-
    land and Virginia counties)

In addition, the EPA says that at least forty-two
areas also have unhealthy air levels of carbon

monoxide. Unlike smog, the most serious carbon monoxide problems occur in the winter. Areas with the most severe carbon monoxide problems include:

1. Los Angeles–Long Beach, California
2. Denver, Colorado
3. Phoenix, Arizona
4. Provo-Orem, Utah
5. Anchorage, Alaska
6. Ft. Collins, Colorado
7. Fairbanks, Alaska
8. Newark, New Jersey
9. Albuquerque, New Mexico
10. Raleigh-Durham, North Carolina
11. Las Vegas, Nevada
12. Medford, Oregon
13. Sacramento, California
14. Greeley, Colorado
15. Reno, Nevada
16. Nashua, New Hampshire
17. New York, New York
18. Boise, Idaho

The counties with the most severe nitrogen dioxide problems are:

1. Davidson (Tennessee)
2. Los Angeles (California)
3. Denver (Colorado)

4. Union (New Jersey)
5. Orange (California)
6. Philadelphia (Pennsylvania)
7. Riverside (California)
8. Washoe (Nevada)
9. Essex (New Jersey)
10. Cook (Illinois)

The EPA says that the following counties can't meet federal health standards for airborne lead:

1. Collin (Texas)
2. Dakota (Minnesota)
3. Douglas (Nebraska)
4. Iron (Missouri)
5. Jefferson (Alabama)
6. Jefferson (Missouri)
7. Lewis and Clark (Montana)
8. Marion (Indiana)
9. Muscogee (Georgia)
10. Shelby (Tennessee)
11. Williamson (Tennessee)

## Other Pollutants

Over the past twenty years, scientists have discovered that the quest for clean, healthy air must extend beyond the initial seven pollutants targeted by the EPA. There are a number of toxic air pollutants—including several carcinogens—that aren't currently regulated.

The EPA has named ten counties with the country's highest levels of toxic air emissions:

1. Los Angeles (California)
2. Cook (Illinois)
3. Harris (Texas)
4. New York (New York)
5. Wayne (Michigan)
6. Dallas (Texas)
7. Orange (California)
8. San Diego (California)
9. Cuyahoga (Ohio)
10. Allegheny (Pennsylvania)

Scientists have also identified a host of other new problems related to air pollution—including global warming and ozone depletion—that government regulatory agencies are now trying to address.

## Are My Children at Risk from Air Pollution

Yes, though in most cases you can minimize that risk. Remember that our air is polluted by dozens of different chemicals, some of which are carcinogens. Most are invisible to the eye. Because children tend to spend a great deal of time outdoors during the summer, the worst part of the smog season, and because they breathe more rapidly than adults, children tend to inhale more of these pollutants. Once in the lungs, these contaminants are absorbed into a child's bloodstream.

Air pollutants can cause shortness of breath, headaches, eye irritation, and, in extreme cases, can permanently diminish lung capacity. Although a definite link has not yet been established, some scientists suspect that a recent rise in asthma cases may be the result of air pollution.

## What Can I Do?

If you live in an urban area and don't already know, find out how health authorities publicize an air pollution (or smog) alert—triggered when conditions are especially unhealthy—then learn the differences in the various kinds of warnings. In some urban areas, warnings are issued in stages depending on the severity of the air quality problem. As parents, you should take precautions any time an alert is sounded, regardless of the stage, because children are so vulnerable.

During the summer especially, you should restrict your child's outdoor activities during certain times of the day. The morning tends to be a healthier period for activity because smog increases through the day as more and more cars take to the roads. Remember too that the very worst days are in the hot summer when humidity traps particulate matter in the air and children often have the most time to play outdoors.

Don't assume that smog is only an urban problem; wind easily distributes air pollutants to the suburbs and beyond. In the Washington, D.C., area, for example, smog problems still exist more than forty miles away from the city limits. Smog has even become a problem in several national parks, even though they are located in remote areas. Nevertheless, for most families living in rural areas, this is one aspect of the air quality problem you probably don't need to worry about. To be certain, call your local health department and ask if your area is meeting federal air quality standards.

## Is Smog My Only Worry?

Unfortunately no, though the public notification of unhealthy conditions makes it the easiest to monitor. There are two other relatively recent problems you should be concerned about.

## Toxic Air Pollutants

One category of pollutants largely ignored by the original Clean Air Act is a class of toxic compounds that enter the atmosphere from a host of commercial and industrial sources. When Congress amended the Clean Air Act in 1990, it took steps to limit these pollutants, although the results of this legislation won't be fully realized until after the turn of the century. But if you do live in an industrialized area, be aware that Congress has also created a mechanism to at least inform you of potential hazards in your community. This federal "right to know" law requires that industries conduct an annual inventory of all toxic emissions.

These toxic release inventories are readily available through local libraries so you can find the names and quantities of pollutants coming from your local industries. If, for example, you lived in Pocatello, Idaho, the inventory would tell you that the largest polluter is the FMC Corporation chemical plant, which pours some 2.3 million pounds of toxic material into the environment each year. Or if you live in Golden, Colorado, the largest source of pollutants is the Coors Brewing Company plant, which discharges 583,000 pounds of chemicals into the air and water annually.

The annual data can also be obtained on your home computer with a floppy disk available from

the EPA, or by modem. For further information
about online access, contact the National Library
of Medicine at (800) 272-4787.

You should realize that the toxic release information has its limitations. While the reports will
tell you the name and quantity of each pollutant
being released, they will not tell you what the risk
is—if any. Nevertheless, it is helpful to at least be
aware of the potential risk so you can do further research on your own.

Using corporate toxic release figures, the EPA
has compiled lists ranking national pollution problems. The states with the largest quantities of toxic
pollutants are:

1. Louisiana
2. Texas
3. Indiana
4. Tennessee
5. Ohio

The EPA reports that the industries releasing
the most toxic waste into the environment are:

1. Chemical manufacturing
2. Primary metals
3. Paper manufacturing
4. Transportation
5. Plastics

## Ozone Depletion

In the 1980s, scientists made an astounding discovery. The upper atmosphere's protective ozone layer (not to be confused with harmful ground-level ozone) had virtually disappeared at the South Pole, creating a seasonal "hole" over Antarctica. The discovery was particularly troublesome because the upper atmosphere's ozone layer filters out cancer-causing ultraviolet sunlight. Though the hole has been largely confined to Antarctica, scientists have since discovered that this protective blanket has thinned over much of the globe.

The major culprit is a class of industrial chemicals called chlorofluorocarbons, or CFCs. These chemicals have been used in a variety of ways: as a common aerosol propellant, a cleaning solvent used by the electronics industry, and a common refrigerant for auto and home air conditioners and refrigerators.

Though treaties have been signed that call for the eventual elimination of CFCs—and many uses have been eliminated—the damaged ozone layer has created potential health risks, particularly for children who spend time outside in the bright sun. Because CFCs have eaten away at the protective ozone layer, all of us are being exposed to higher levels of ultraviolet sunlight. Such exposures raise the risk of skin cancer and eye damage, particularly cataract formation.

## What Should I Do About This Problem?

The answer is not to spend the rest of our lives indoors. Sunlight is healthy—and necessary—because it helps the body produce vitamin D, which is essential for cell growth. But overexposure can lead to skin cancer, eye problems, and even impaired immune systems.

Unfortunately, we live in a culture that still regards a deep, dark tan as a sign of radiant good health; our sense of fashion still seems to triumph over the increasingly dire warnings that too much sun is bad for us. Scientists now know that even one severe sunburn—the blistering, peeling kind—can set the stage for adult skin cancer, which can be deadly. Children, with their thinner skin and penchant for spending more time outdoors, are generally at greater risk than adults.

The key to protection from UV radiation is moderation. First, remember that children with certain physical characteristics may face a higher risk. If your child has blond or red hair and a fair complexion, he or she is more likely to get sunburned. Conversely, dark-skinned children face a lower risk because of a skin pigment, melanin, that offers some natural protection from ultraviolet rays.

Regardless of your child's hair and skin color,

there are some precautions you as parents should take.

You should dress your children in protective clothing, including long-sleeved shirts, long pants, and hats, which help protect eyes from ultraviolet light. Cotton offers the best balance between protection and comfort, although white cotton shirts let in a lot of UV light when dry and significantly more when wet.

Sunglasses help protect eyes from UV damage, *if* your child will wear them, though inexpensive children's glasses provide little protection. Dark lenses are best, and some brands will even tell you how effective they are in screening ultraviolet rays. Most opticians can chemically treat your child's sunglasses for greater UV protection. The cost is twenty-five to thirty dollars, but it may be worth the investment if your child is, for example, involved in sports that involve many hours outdoors. More manufacturers are making children's sunglasses that offer significant UV protection.

You can also have your child wear a sunscreen whenever he or she is outdoors. If your child plays near water, use waterproof sunscreen and reapply it frequently. Remember, UV exposure is a problem even on cloudy days. Regardless of the cloud cover, midday is the worst time; the sun's rays are strongest from ten in the morning until three in the afternoon. Restricting exposure to morning or late afternoon is your best bet. Also, be aware that UV risk isn't confined to the summertime; you should also be cautious in the fall, winter, and spring because the ozone layer is thinnest in cold weather.

Sunscreens are rated according to a numerical system called the sun protection factor (SPF). A sunblock with SPF 20, for example, will allow a fair-skinned person to stay in the sun twenty times longer than usual without sunburn. For most fair-skinned children, burning could start within fifteen or twenty minutes without any protection, so a sunblock with SPF 20 would mean at least six hours outside without risk of sunburn. For children, select sunscreens with an SPF of at least 15. Some companies make sunscreens of up to SPF 45 intended specifically for children.

When choosing a sunscreen, select one that filters out both UVA and UVB sunlight. Otherwise, most sunscreens use essentially the same ingredients. One caution: for children, avoid sunscreens with avobenzone (Parsol) because it might irritate tender skin, and be careful when applying any sunscreen near a child's eyes. Sunscreen should not be used on infants under six months. For the youngest infants and toddlers, protective clothing—and umbrellas—are the safest alternatives. Make sure your stroller or carriage has a protective bonnet, parasol, or hood to shield your child from the sun's rays.

The National Weather Service has begun issuing a new daily solar warning index that operates on a scale from 0 to 10 and above to indicate the risk of exposure to UV radiation. A low rating indicates minimal risk; a rating of 10 or higher carries a higher risk. The system is in effect in fewer than sixty cities so far, but may be expanded soon.

## Indoor Air Quality

As serious as the outdoor pollution problem seems, many experts feel that the greatest air quality risk may be inside your home. In fact, EPA experts from all over the nation wrote a report in 1989 detailing what they considered the biggest threats to human health. Topping the list: indoor air pollution. It was thus no real surprise when the EPA released a report in early 1993 claiming that secondhand cigarette smoke may be responsible for three thousand cancer deaths a year—a greater risk to infants and children than all of the toxic air pollutants released by the nation's factories combined.

## Smoke

Secondhand tobacco smoke has long been recognized as a major cause of death and disease, including respiratory and heart problems and lung cancer among smokers. Increasingly, medical experts have recognized that nonsmokers are at risk when they are exposed to secondhand smoke from cigarettes, pipes, and cigars. The EPA reports that cigarette smoke contains over four thousand different substances, including forty-three known carcinogens. Many of these chemicals can cause respiratory problems and eye irritation.

Looking specifically at the risks to the children, the EPA concluded:

- Perhaps as many as 1 million children have more frequent and severe asthma attacks because of inhaling secondhand smoke. Smoke can trigger an asthma attack even in a previously asthma-free child.
- Inhaling secondhand smoke increases the risk of lower-respiratory-tract infections (like bronchitis or pneumonia) in infants and young children. The report estimated that as many as three hundred thousand cases of respiratory infections annually may be caused by secondhand smoke.
- Exposure to secondhand smoke increases the likelihood of fluid in the inner ear along with other symptoms of upper-respiratory-tract infections.

The experts at the EPA feel that exposure to passive smoke may be *the most significant environmental risk facing children.* One of the wisest things you can do as a parent is to minimize your child's exposure to secondhand smoke. If you are a smoker, perhaps the most meaningful contribution you can make to your family's health is to avoid smoking in your home or car—or wherever else there is a chance of exposure. (Obviously, it's best for your health to quit.) If you aren't a smoker, make certain to avoid (whenever practical) other situations where your children might be exposed to secondhand smoke. Declare your home a smoke-free environment. Make smoking visitors go outdoors (being exiled might even get them to quit!).

## Other Indoor Air Problems

In addition to secondhand smoke, there are a number of other potential air quality problems in your home.

How would you recognize the problem? The American Lung Association says that the symptoms of exposure—dizziness, nausea, eye or skin irritation—usually disappear when you go outside. If you have any of these symptoms, you may have an indoor air problem.

Our homes can (and often do) harbor a number of potentially hazardous pollutants from a variety of sources, including heating and cooling systems, appliances, fireplaces, and even drapes, wallcoverings, and carpeting. Unfortunately, the emphasis on more energy-efficient homes (and offices) has inadvertently contributed to the problem by reducing the amount of fresh air circulating through the buildings we live and work in. The situation has been further aggravated by emissions from certain building materials and decorative items. Among the chemicals causing concern:

*Carbon Monoxide*

Carbon monoxide is a colorless, odorless gas that is most commonly emitted as a by-product of combustion in wood stoves, fireplaces, and unvented kerosene heaters. It can also be emitted from malfunctioning furnaces, water heaters, gas dryers, and kitchen stoves. Homeowners with attached garages should also be aware that running cars or lawn mowers in the garage can build up carbon monoxide in the home.

The symptoms of carbon monoxide exposure are impeded coordination, fatigue, headaches, and nausea. At high levels, carbon monoxide poisoning can be fatal.

To guard against carbon monoxide poisoning, have your gas-powered appliances, furnaces, and water heaters checked at least once a year. Make sure your stoves and heaters are properly vented to the outside. Never leave your car running in the garage with the garage door closed, particularly when young children are inside the car or garage.

Carbon monoxide is an insidious poison whose symptoms can creep up unnoticed. Sadly, there is an increasing number of news reports of children dying in their sleep from this invisible hazard. Public awareness of this threat was greatly increased in the summer of 1994, when former tennis star and sports commentator Vitas Gerulaitis died from accidental carbon monoxide poisoning. As a result of increased sensitivity to this risk, some cities, including Chicago, have mandated the installation of carbon monoxide detectors in homes and apartment buildings. It's a good idea to install these detectors in your home—they are available at many hardware stores—and to maintain and check them regularly, just as you would your smoke detectors. For information on detectors, write: Consumer Product Safety Commission, Washington, D.C. 20207.

### Nitrogen Dioxide

Nitrogen dioxide is a common outdoor pollutant that can also be found in the home. Many of its sources are the same as those for carbon monoxide: gas appliances, furnaces, woodstoves, etc. The symptoms of nitrogen dioxide exposure are eye and respiratory irritation. Long-term exposure to even low levels can cause bronchitis.

To avoid inhaling nitrogen dioxide fumes, don't use your gas oven to heat your home. Make sure appliances are properly vented and maintained. Use an exhaust fan while cooking.

*Formaldehyde*

This pungent-smelling gas is present in cigarette smoke and dozens of common household products. It has been used in the resins in particle board, plywood paneling, and in adhesives used for making drapes and carpeting, although manufacturers are now making products with lower-emitting formaldehyde.

Urea formaldehyde foam insulation—an older product no longer widely used—is also a source. If your home was insulated with a spray foam between 1973 and 1983, it is possible that formaldehyde foam was used. Telltale signs of this insulation are a crusty, powdery substance around electrical outlets or window frames. Even if your home contains urea formaldehyde foam, it does not automatically mean you have a problem. Emissions are highest immediately after installation; after that, they diminish gradually.

The symptoms of formaldehyde exposure include lethargy, rashes, nausea, and respiratory, skin, and eye irritation. High levels can trigger asthma attacks. If you suspect a problem, there are formaldehyde detector kits available for home use, or you can have your air tested by an expert. Call your local EPA office for the name of a qualified professional. For children, airborne formaldehyde levels should probably not exceed 0.05 parts per million.

The best way to remedy a formaldehyde problem is to increase ventilation. You can also seal wall areas and other sources of gas with sealants, caulking, or coatings. Remember that high temperature and humidity will speed the release of formaldehyde gas. When buying new building materials, specify low-emitting products. To control low-level emissions, use an air purifier that contains chemically active filtering materials such as potassium permanganate.

In extreme cases, experts can use ammonia fumigation to reduce formaldehyde levels. Your home will be sealed after you and your family have evacuated it and will then be filled with ammonia hydroxide. The ammonia reacts with formaldehyde, creating harmless byproducts. This procedure has been known to reduce formaldehyde levels by as much as 90 percent.

### Radon

Radon is a colorless, odorless radioactive gas given off by soil or rock formations containing trace levels of uranium. It can enter your home through cracks or openings in the foundation but also can be transported by drinking water.

According to the EPA, radon gas is the second leading cause of lung cancer (cigarettes are first) and may be responsible for 20,000 deaths annually.

Nearly every area of the country is plagued with radon problems, but the distribution of the gas doesn't follow any pattern. In one New Jersey neighborhood, a home had so much radon gas that living in it carried a risk equivalent to smoking ten packs of cigarettes a day. The residents next door had no problems at all.

The fastest way to find out whether you're family is being exposed to radon is to check your home with an inexpensive radon test kit, available from your local hardware store for about twenty dollars. You should do the test during the winter months when the house is closed up and the radon levels are at their highest. The test is easy to do: you set up the monitor for a specified period of time (from one week to one month), then mail it in to an EPA-approved laboratory for analysis. Normally, the detector should be placed in the basement, where radon levels are highest. If you are concerned about the accuracy of a do-it-yourself test, you can hire a professional tester. This option is probably the best if you need to verify the results before you can sell your home. If you do decide to hire a professional, make certain you select one who has passed the EPA proficiency test. Although this is not an endorsement from the EPA, it does mean that the technician meets minimum federal standards.

Many parts of the country now require radon tests when you sell your home. Even if this isn't a requirement in your area, you should demand a certified radon test before you buy a new home.

Radon levels are measured in picocuries per liter (pCi/l). The EPA considers anything above 4 pCi/l to be cause for concern. If your tests are above 200 pCi/l, you should consider relocating your family until the home can be retested and repaired.

If you find a problem, don't panic. First, retest to make certain the first results were accurate. If the second test is also high, simple procedures such as repairing cracks, sealing foundations, and improving ventilation will often solve the problem, according to the EPA. If you have radon in your water, which a professional can determine, a treatment system may be necessary. The EPA's booklet "Radon Reduction Methods: A Homeowner's Guide," available from EPA, Washington, D.C. 20460, is a valuable tool for understanding your options.

### Lead
In older homes, deteriorating lead paint can release lead particles into the air. Consult chapter 1 for more information on identifying and correcting lead hazards.

### Asbestos
Asbestos is a grayish white mineral fiber that was used widely before 1970 in an array of products including roofing, ceilings, flooring, acoustic paneling materials, and insulation. In older homes, it was often used to insulate plumbing, furnace ducts, and even some appliances.

When asbestos crumbles, it unleashes tiny fibers into the air. These fibers can cause major health problems, including lung cancer, malignant mesothelioma (a cancer of the chest and intestinal tissues), and asbestosis, an irreversible scarring of lung tissue. Each year some ten thousand people die from exposure to asbestos, exposure that often occurred decades earlier. Armed with the knowledge of asbestos's toxic effects, the EPA banned most uses of this insulator.

It can be alarming to discover that your home contains asbestos. You may find it around the pipes in your basement, inside your furnace door, beneath the linoleum in your kitchen, and elsewhere. Fortunately, asbestos is only a risk to your family if it is crumbling and flaking or if it is disturbed for any reason. Undisturbed or adequately sealed, it poses no risk.

I don't advise you to go poking around the pipes to see if you have asbestos; if you suspect there may be a problem leave that to the professionals. If you do have asbestos in your home, your chief decision is whether to seal it or have it removed. In either case, the decision should be made with the help of a qualified professional, and the work should be performed by someone specifically trained and licensed in asbestos abatement. I must emphasize that the real risk here lies in improper asbestos removal, which can scatter the fibers, thereby creating the very exposure you want to avoid. If the asbestos in your home appears to be deteriorating or must be removed for renovation purposes, do not attempt the task yourself. Both your local health department and the nearest EPA office can provide you with a list of qualified contractors from which to choose.

Removal is a complicated process. You and your family will have to relocate while the work is done. Qualified technicians will perform the task wearing protective clothing and approved respiration equipment. As part of the job, they will test the air after the work is completed to make certain levels are safe.

If you are in the process of looking for a new home or apartment, it's a good idea to have an independent inspector check the premises to assess the asbestos situation. You should be aware of any need for asbestos abatement before you make a buying—or selling—decision.

### Biological Pollutants

Household air is full of tiny biological contaminants, including bacteria, viruses, spores, pollen, animal dander, fungi, and other microscopic pollutants. Some may carry communicable diseases; others may trigger allergic reactions or asthma attacks. These tiny biological particles can be spread throughout a home through the heating, cooling, and ventilation systems and are often stirred up by activities such as vacuuming.

The telltale signs of such pollutants are: a stale or moldy odor in the air; moisture condensing on windows; moldy carpeting, walls, or furniture; or excessive dust. The symptoms of airborne biological pollutants include eye, ear, nose, and throat irritation; asthma; and hay fever.

If you find you have this problem, the first step is to keep indoor humidity levels between 30 and 50 percent. In the winter, use a humidifier if necessary since moisture helps promote growth. In warmer weather, you may need a dehumidifier to remove excess moisture from the air. Installing exhaust fans in damp areas such as the bathroom will also help reduce humidity levels through the rest of your home.

If you use humidifiers, a cold air model may be best. Some humidifiers may inadvertently help disperse spores, etc., by breaking matter up into smaller particles that can then get deeper inside the lungs. Make sure that any water used in a humidifier is scrupulously clean. Use distilled water and dump out the excess every day and scrub out the water tank to prevent mold or other contaminants from growing. Likewise, dispose of the water in dehumidifier tanks before it creates a stagnant breeding ground for microbes.

Keep attics and basements well ventilated. Try to keep your home (especially a child's play area and bedroom) as dust-free as possible. Many parents find that their children react with strong allergic responses to the dust mites that routinely inhabit carpets, bedding, rugs, and drapes. If your child is tremendously allergic, there may be no other remedy but to eliminate the dust mites' breeding sites by pulling up rugs and carpets, taking down drapes, cleaning bed, stuffed animals, drapes, and bedding.

Though the range of possibilities may be a little daunting, you can minimize the dangers to your family by following some basic guidelines.

# CHECKLIST

☐ Familiarize yourself with the smog alert system in your area so that you can keep your children indoors when necessary.

☐ Protect your children from excessive ultraviolet radiation by using sunscreen and dressing them in protective clothing.

☐ Give your children a smoke-free environment.

☐ Have experts inspect your home to make certain you have adequate ventilation.

☐ Install carbon monoxide detectors and change their batteries twice a year as you do with smoke detectors.

☐ Have your home tested for radon and take any necessary measures to correct the problem if levels are too high.

❑ Have your home inspected for asbestos and hire a qualified professional to perform any necessary asbestos abatement.

❑ Take measures to keep your home as clean, dust-free, and well ventilated as possible to reduce the proliferation of molds, funguses, and other biological irritants.

## RESOURCES

### For More Information

EPA Asbestos Hotline: (800) 368-5888. For questions about asbestos in homes or schools.

EPA Toxic Substances Hotline: (202) 554-1404. For information on testing laboratories.

### Publications

*Asbestos in Your Home,* a booklet by the EPA and the Consumer Product Safety Commission. To order call (800) 638-CPSC.

*The Nontoxic Home and Office* by Debra Lynn Dadd, Jeremy P. Tarcher, Inc., 1992.

# Water Pollution

**M**ore than two decades ago, the *Chicago Tribune* astounded its midwestern readers with a tale about Great Lakes water pollution that seemed almost unbelievable. In a Sunday magazine feature, veteran environmental reporter Casey Bukro documented the waterway's sad legacy of pollution from municipal sewage and industrial waste. Michigan's Rouge River was so polluted it was the color of a brilliant sunset; Cleveland's Cuyahoga River regularly caught fire because of the massive quantities of flammable chemicals that industry had dumped into the water. Along much of the shoreline of Lakes Michigan, Erie, and Ontario, swimming was prohibited because the water contained untreated municipal sewage that had dramatically elevated the levels of disease-causing bacteria. The prognosis for the area's waterways was so grim that several experts began writing obituaries, declaring the lakes dead—certainly beyond any hope of salvation.

Fortunately, the waterways weren't dead— though they were definitely in the intensive care unit. Congress moved in with an aggressive new Clean Water Act, which aimed to corral both municipal and industrial waste. It also authorized billions of dollars in federal grants to build new municipal water treatment plants and the necessary sewage pipelines to connect homes and businesses. States responded with aggressive new regulatory and enforcement efforts. Within years, the nation's rivers, lakes, and streams responded to this onslaught of attention. Beaches reopened; Lake Erie, once declared dead, rebounded spectacularly. The Cuyahoga stopped burning; the Rouge lost its reddish sheen. Fish even ventured back into the once-desolate waters.

Even as great strides were being made in cleaning up the waterways, scientists came to the dismaying conclusion that water pollution, like air pollution, was a much more complicated problem than they had originally thought. New, totally unregulated sources of water pollution were discovered. When the highly toxic pollutant 2,3,7,8-TCDD (dioxin) showed up in a remote area of the northern Great Lakes, scientists discovered to their horror that it had been transported by air from industrial sources hundreds of miles away. It was also discovered that fertilizer and pesticide runoff from farms was sapping the life from many of the nation's waterways, including Florida's Everglades, the Chesapeake Bay, and California's San Francisco Bay. Scientists learned to their amazement that some pollutants—carcinogenic pesticides, for example—were still causing extensive and perhaps irreversible damage despite aggressive regulatory efforts. On Long Island, for example, nearly one well in four was found to contain unsafe levels of aldicarb, a highly toxic pesticide once used extensively on the island's potato crops. And despite an investment of billions of dollars in new sewage treatment plants, hundreds of beaches nationwide are still closed each summer because of high bacteria levels—a direct result of improperly treated (or untreated) sewage being discharged into our waterways.

So what does this mean for concerned parents? It means diligence is necessary, because water quality—particularly for drinking water—does occasionally pose a health risk to your children. They are especially vulnerable to water pollution, partly because they tend to drink more water than adults, partly because their developing organs are more susceptible to the poisons that sometimes contaminate our water supplies.

## Drinking Water Safety

Every public water supply in the United States serving twenty-five or more households is regulated by the EPA under the Safe Drinking Water Act, a law that sets maximum safe limits for contaminants and provides enforcement steps for any system not meeting the standards. Though this protection would seem adequate, there are shortcomings:

- Approximately 40 million people use water from private wells, which aren't covered by the law.
- Public systems don't always comply with the law and enforcement has been lax.
- Some pollutants aren't covered under the act.

Without overstating the risk, you should be aware that in a 1990 survey of EPA experts, contaminated drinking water was one of the few environmental problems they listed in the "high health risk" category. An overview of the regulatory system might help explain why the EPA regulators feel there is some risk.

## Primary Drinking Water Standards

The Safe Drinking Water Act sets both primary and secondary standards (called maximum contaminant levels, or MCLs) for drinking water pollutants.

Primary drinking water standards regulate the pollutants considered the greatest threat to public health. They include limits on the following pollutants:

### Coliform Bacteria

Coliform bacteria come from human or animal fecal matter. These can cause a range of illnesses, including dysentery, hepatitis, and cholera, along with a host of gastroenteric problems.

### Cryptosporidium

Cryptosporidium is a microscopic parasite that was responsible for one of the largest waterborne disease outbreaks in modern U.S. history. In 1993, more than a hundred Milwaukee residents died and thousands of others were sickened by a city water supply that was contaminated by cryptosporidium, which is often found in polluted farm runoff.

Symptoms of the illness—called cryptosporidiosis—include nausea, stomach cramps, diarrhea, and severe dehydration. Some symptoms can linger up to three weeks.

Cryptosporidium is especially troublesome because it is resistant to chlorination, the primary method of water purification in many cities.

Though the Milwaukee incident has prompted stricter water quality monitoring, environmentalists say cryptosporidium will remain a threat until treatment plants are upgraded or the source of the problem is eliminated.

### Nitrates

Nitrates commonly enter the water supply as runoff from land treated with industrial fertilizers. They can react with oxygen-carrying hemoglobin in the blood to cause a circulatory condition called "blue baby syndrome." Infants from six to twelve months old are most vulnerable to this disorder.

### Inorganic Chemicals

These chemicals include arsenic, barium, cadmium, lead, mercury, selenium, silver, and naturally occurring fluoride. The contaminants can cause a wide range of medical problems, including liver and kidney problems, nervous system damage, and circulatory problems. Lead is of particular concern because children are especially vulnerable. Even minimal exposure can inhibit mental development (see chapter 1 for more details).

## Organic Chemicals

Most of the organic chemical standards involve contaminants commonly found in water supplies: Endrin, lindane, methoxychlor, 2,4-D, and trichloroethylene (TCE). Some of these pollutants are carcinogens; others can cause nervous system problems or liver and kidney damage. Other regulated organic chemicals include benzene, a carcinogen found in petroleum products and industrial solvents, and vinyl chloride, a carcinogen found in a variety of synthetic products.

## Radionuclides

Three common radioactive substances—all carcinogens—are also regulated. The radioactive substance that isn't regulated is radon. Its presence in your water supply is really not as big a problem as its effects as an air pollutant (see chapter 4).

### Trihalomethanes (THMs)

These suspected carcinogens are formed when chlorine (a common disinfectant used to treat water) reacts with certain organic pollutants commonly found in water systems. There are two important factors to remember when it comes to THMs: First, the longer the chlorine comes in contact with organic pollutants, the higher the levels of THMs. Thus THM levels rise as water travels through the distribution system. Second, THM levels are highest in warm weather, when extra chlorine is added at water treatment plants to overcome taste and odor problems caused by the bacteria that thrive in warm weather.

Expectant mothers should be as concerned about THMs as the parents of young children. A 1993 study by the U.S. Public Health Service found that exposure to THMs slightly increased the risk of having premature or low-birthweight babies. And, though the federal THM limit is 100 parts per billion (ppb), the study found that exposure to THM concentrations of 80 ppb or greater also increased the risk of birth defects.

## Secondary Drinking Water Standards

These standards are less important from a public health standpoint, but are essential for maintain-

ing taste, hardness, and other aesthetic characteristics of the water supply.

## pH

Standards have been set for water pH, a measure of
acidity. Extreme pH levels—either acid or alka-
line—can negatively affect taste.

## Chloride

Chloride levels can also influence water's taste and
its corrosive characteristics. Too much chloride, for
example, can cause browning of teeth.

## Copper

Copper standards are imposed mostly for reasons
of taste and color.

## Sulfate

Sulfate standards are imposed mostly for reasons
of taste, although excessive quantities of sulfate
can have a laxative effect.

## Total Dissolved Solids

This is a standard that regulates the hardness of water. Excessive hardness can damage plumbing and limit the effectiveness of soaps.

## Do These Standards Mean My Water Is Safe?

Unfortunately, no. Water system operators are supposed to test their water regularly for the chemicals listed in the standards and report the results to the EPA (or the state environmental agency, acting as an EPA surrogate). The fallacy in this system, according to an EPA report, is that enforcement of standards is "virtually nonexistent." The report also noted that water supply operators, although required to notify the public of violations, often fail to do so. If you have any questions about water quality in your community, call the local water department. Test results are public information under all circumstances.

According to Benjamin Goldman's book *The Truth About Where You Live,* the counties showing the most frequent violations of Safe Drinking Water Act standards are:

1. Harris (Texas)
2. Cambria (Pennsylvania)
3. Luzerne (Pennsylvania)

4. McLennan (Texas)
5. Berkshire (Massachusetts)
6. San Bernardino (California)
7. Clinton (Pennsylvania)
8. Ellis (Texas)
9. Kings (California)
10. Centre (Pennsylvania)

Another major problem with the Safe Drinking Water Act is that only a minute number of possible pollutants are covered. Tests have shown literally hundreds of different pollutants in some water systems. The law also exempts systems that don't provide drinking water year round, which means that some summer camps and residential and resort areas escape regulation altogether.

## How Is Drinking Water Treated?

Regardless of the source of their water (surface or underground) most public treatment plants operate in a similar manner. Incoming water is filtered to remove floating debris, then chemicals are added to create particles called floc that collect solids suspended in the water. The water is gently agitated in huge holding basins, causing the floc particles to cling together. After agitation, the water sits long enough for the particles to settle to the bottom.

The water is then pumped through a filtration system (granulated carbon is the most effective). Next, chemicals (commonly chlorine or alum) are added to kill disease-carrying bacteria. Other chemicals may be added for corrosion control. In many cities, fluoride also is added to reduce tooth decay.

Other steps are sometimes used to correct specific problems. For example, aeration (pumping air through the water) is performed to remove pollutants called volatile organic compounds, which evaporate when exposed to air.

After treatment, the water is pumped through a network of pipes that often extend miles from the treatment plant to homes. Some communities also use huge storage tanks (often mounted on stiltlike structures) to hold treated water.

## What Can I Do About Drinking Water Safety?

If you are getting water through a municipal system, federal law gives you the right to ask for the following information:

- Results of a recent laboratory analysis of the water.
- List of the contaminants routinely tested.
- Indications if any of the contaminants exceed federal standards.

■ Method of notification if violations of federal standards are found.

■ Description of the method of treatment.

■ Results of any tests of lead levels.

To ask for this information, find the number of your water department (or public works department) in the telephone directory or on your most recent water bill.

If your water is coming from a private well, it might be worth the expense to have it tested by a private laboratory. A good comprehensive test (including tests for bacteria, lead, and some of the most common organic and inorganic pollutants) will cost at least two hundred dollars. These tests can also be done by mail, although shipping charges could add thirty dollars to the price. The mail-order lab will send you a kit with sterile bottles and instructions. You draw the samples, then send them back to the lab by overnight mail (otherwise, bacteria readings won't be accurate). Results will be mailed back to you in four to six weeks. *Consumer Reports* recommends three mail-order labs: WaterTest, National Testing Laboratories, and Suburban Water Testing (see the resources section at the end of the chapter for addresses). If you can't locate an EPA certified laboratory (or don't want to use mail order), call the EPA drinking water hotline for recommendations at (800) 426-4791.

Unfortunately, the cost of a laboratory analysis

for all pollutants would be prohibitive, so *Consumer Reports* suggests that you be selective:

- Always test for bacteria, radon, and inorganic chemicals.
- Test for lead if your home is more than thirty years old.
- Test for nitrates and pesticides if you live in a farming community.
- Test for organic chemicals if you live within two miles of a gas station, refinery, landfill, chemical plant, petroleum refinery, or military base.

## What About Home Treatment Systems?

Be aware that the EPA does not certify or recommend any home water treatment system, though independent groups say that some of these appliances can be effective for purifying water under certain circumstances.

### Reverse Osmosis Systems

In a reverse osmosis system, water is forced through a membrane, which is reasonably effective at removing inorganic chemicals such as nitrates and lead. Such systems can also improve taste and odor. Some are countertop models; the most expensive are installed as an integral part of your home's plumbing system. Costs range from several hundred to several thousand dollars. For countertop units, *Consumer Reports* recommends the Culligan Aqua Cleer Compact. The best-rated under-counter systems were the Culligan Aqua Cleer and Everpure Ultimate 1.

## Activated Carbon Filters

Activated carbon systems are most effective for removing organic contaminants and should only be used where water has already been disinfected. Though some filters attach to the faucet or showerhead, the most effective models are installed under the counter in the water line. The filters must be changed frequently because they have limited holding capacity and can become a haven for bacteria if not serviced regularly. Though the under-the-counter system works best for filtering drinking water, a carbon filter on your showerhead will cut down on chemicals and radon that volatilize and become air pollutants. Under-the-counter models can usually be purchased for less than three hundred dollars; faucet or showerhead filters are usually less than thirty dollars.

*Consumer Reports* recommends the Ametek

CCF-201 (also sold as Sears 34201), the Ecowater Master, the Amway 9230, or the Hurley II filters.

### Distillation Systems

Distillers remove bacteria and inorganic chemicals but are less effective with pesticides and organic chemicals. They are also slow, require frequent filter changes, and can affect the taste of water. Because of these drawbacks, you should turn to distillation only if you want to remove metals from your water.

Most units cost more than three hundred dollars. *Consumer Reports* recommends the Aqua Clean Model 4 or Sears 34555, which is roughly half the cost and equally as effective.

When purchasing any treatment unit, buy from a reputable dealer (one who is a member of the Water Quality Association). You must also read sales literature carefully; it should list the specific contaminants the system will remove.

## What About Bottled Water?

Bottled water is not necessarily superior to tap water for several reasons. It is regulated by the Food and Drug Administration—not the EPA—under guidelines that aren't as strict as those of the Safe Drinking Water Act. Though many companies claim their water comes from pristine mountain springs, in fact one brand in four comes from the tap. The FDA tested bottled water in 1991 and found high bacteria levels in 31 percent of the brands tested. If you do decide to use bottled water, find a brand that guarantees it meets Safe Drinking Water Act standards. In general, domestic brands are better since imported water is rarely tested at the border.

## Surface Water Safety

Parents need to be diligent about surface water quality for two primary reasons: swimming and consuming freshwater fish.

### Swimming

Each summer, health authorities are forced to close beaches, primarily because of high coliform bacteria counts, which are usually the result of sewage in the waterway. As mentioned earlier, these bacteria can cause a host of illnesses, including dysentery, hepatitis, and cholera, along with a number of common gastroenteric infections. Though few of these diseases are considered life-threatening with proper treatment, they can cause an awful lot of discomfort for a youngster and his or her parents (not to mention medical expenses).

The easiest way to avoid bacteria-laden water is to abide by any health advisories that are issued during the course of the summer. If you have any qualms (or questions), call your local health department.

In the late 1980s, a number of beaches—many of them in the mid-Atlantic states—were plagued with medical wastes washing ashore. Needless to say, the presence of used hypodermic needles and other medical garbage posed a significant health threat. Though stricter disposal laws have reduced the amount of medical wastes on the nation's beaches, you should always be on the lookout. And even though children love running barefoot in the sand, it would not be a bad idea to encourage your children to wear water sandals when they are walking and playing on the beach.

### Eating Fish or Shellfish

Parents should always be extremely cautious when it comes to consuming fish from any of the nation's freshwater rivers, lakes, or streams. Many of these waterways have been tainted by pesticides and metals (like mercury), making the fish unsafe for children and pregnant women. See chapter 2 for more details about health advisories for eating fish and shellfish. If you have any doubts, call your local health department first.

# C H E C K L I S T

☐ Test your drinking water for levels of key contaminants.

☐ If necessary, purchase a water treatment system or buy bottled water for drinking, cooking, and preparing baby formula. Check with the FDA for a list of acceptable bottled water manufacturers.

☐ Pay attention to local health advisories and keep your children away from public beaches when necessary.

☐ Have your children wear beach sandals to avoid exposure to organic debris, broken glass, and medical waste.

☐ Avoid fish and shellfish not considered acceptable by your local health department.

## RESOURCES

### For More Information

EPA Safe Drinking Water Hotline: (800) 426-4791. In the District of Columbia and Alaska, call (202) 260-5533.

You can call for advice on a certified testing lab near you or to have other questions about drinking water answered.

Water Quality Association, 4151 Naperville Road, Lisle, IL 60532, (708) 505-0160. Will provide a list of WQA certified water treatment system dealers.

## Testing Services

National Testing Laboratories, 6151 Wilson Mills Road, Cleveland, OH 44143, (800) 458-3330. Also does mail-order testing.

Suburban Water Testing Laboratories, 4600 Kutztown Road, Temple, PA 19560, (800) 433-6595.

WaterTest Corporation of America, 33 South Commercial Street, Manchester, NH 03101, (800) 433-6595. Does mail-order water testing.

## Publications

*The Truth About Where You Live* by Benjamin A. Goldman, Times Books, 1991.

# Other Hazards

**E** nvironmental risks—or any hazards for that matter—don't fit in nice neat compartments. As a parent, your concerns extend beyond pollutants that invade the air, water, and soil. Although the major environmental problems have been covered in the five previous chapters, there are other hazards lurking about that you should be aware of. Many of these hazards are in your home and most represent potential problems, particularly if your children are very young. And that risk doesn't end when your children leave for school in the morning: the classroom can also harbor hazards you'll need to monitor carefully.

## Art Supplies

Most children love art activities, whether it is coloring, drawing, or sculpting with clay. Most schools, preschools, and day care centers are generally careful with the materials they give children, if for no other reason than to comply with a federal law requiring nontoxic art supplies, a regulation that generally covers classrooms up to sixth grade.

MEETS PERFORMANCE STANDARD #
CONFORMS TO ASTM D-4236

CONFORMS TO ASTM D-4236

Parents need to be just as diligent with the art supplies they bring into their homes. Art supplies are labeled according to toxicity, and you should pay attention to those labels when you shop. For starters, look for an Arts and Crafts Materials Institute (ACMI) label (see above). The designations AP (approved product) Nontoxic; CP (certified product) Nontoxic; and Health Label Nontoxic all indicate products safe for children of all ages—even preschoolers. Essentially, these label designations mean that little harm will result if any of these products are ingested, inhaled, or rubbed on the

skin. In addition, a federal label requirement specifies that all art supplies must list any hazardous
ingredients and specify if the product is unfit for
use by children. Other tips:

- In general, you should not let any child under
  the age of twelve use professional art supplies.
- Avoid solvent-based products; use water-
  based products instead.
- Don't use aerosols or dry powders, which can
  be inhaled.
- If you need a solvent to clean up after oil-
  based paints, look for one that carries ACMI
  approval.
- Don't let children use professional pottery
  glazes; some contain lead. Any glaze with an
  ACMI designation of AP or CP would not contain lead.
- Don't let young children use airplane glue,
  epoxy, or any of the fast-bonding adhesives.
  Elmer's School Glue is a good alternative,
  along with a number of pastes.

### What About Other Artists in the Family?

If Mom, Dad, an older sibling, or someone else in
the household happens to be an artist or craftsper-
son, care should be taken to avoid needlessly exposing youngsters to their toxic craft supplies.

The typical art studio is filled with materials that represent a risk to children (and adults, too). Metals like lead, mercury, and cadmium are commonly found in pigments used to make glazes and paint. Solvents like turpentine can be fatal to children even in small doses. Silica dust from pottery making can cause respiratory problems. How serious is the risk? For children, it is minimal if care is exercised to keep them from being exposed. The same is not true, unfortunately, for grown-ups. At least one study has found elevated cancer rates among professional artists.

## Common Poisons

Conscientious parents take steps to child-proof their homes, though, in many cases those efforts focus on the physical hazards that represent potential sources of injury. A recent study of childhood poisonings suggests that some of the greatest risks facing your children may come not from physical injury but from the accidental ingestion of a poison. It certainly seems to make sense, given a young child's penchant for putting nearly anything in his or her mouth.

A 1992 study in the medical journal *Pediatrics* found that some of the most significant sources of childhood poisoning are everyday items in your home that could escape the usual child-proofing regimen. In an analysis of nearly 4 million poisoning cases over eight years, the scientists reached the following conclusions:

- Iron supplements are the leading cause of death. Apparently, children mistake the bright-colored pills for candy.
- Next to iron pills, the most frequent cause of poisoning death was pesticide ingestion. A nearly equal number of children died after swallowing hydrocarbons, like kerosene or lamp oil, which is often scented to provide a pleasant burning odor. Unfortunately, the sweet scent masks the true hazard.
- Also causing a significant number of deaths: cleaning products, gun bluing, analgesics, aspirin, and a host of other adult medications, including antidepressants, antihistamines, and sedatives.
- Though not always fatal, the three most commonly ingested poisons were cosmetics and other personal-care products (including mouthwash), cleaning substances, and plants (see the section on plants later in this chapter).

## Poisonous Household Products

Parents of young children must be especially diligent to protect against poisoning, for the average home is filled with potential hazards. First-time parents need to take special care to child-proof a home that was once the exclusive domain of grown-ups.

Bathrooms, closets, and cabinets are potential minefields when it comes to a child's safety. Among the poison risks:

All aerosol cans
Antiseptics
Aspirin
Bath salts, oil
Cosmetics
Deodorizers, air fresheners
Detergents, fabric softeners, bleach
Disinfectant
Drain cleaner
Flea powders and flea collars
Furniture polish
Hair treatments, including shampoos, rinses
Laxatives
Mothballs
Mouthwash
Nail polish and remover
Ointments
Perfumes, colognes
Petroleum jelly
Prescription drugs
Rubbing alcohol
Scouring powder
Shaving cream

Tile, tub cleaners
Toilet bowl cleaner
Vitamins, mineral supplements
Waxes
Window, rug cleaners

In the basement, garage, or shed, the following should be locked up or otherwise kept from children:

Charcoal fire starter
Fertilizers
Gasoline
Kerosene
Metal cleaners
Paint strippers
Paint thinner
Pesticides
Plant seeds and bulbs
Rodent or insect poisons
Turpentine
Waxes, other car cleaning materials

## Start Your Own Poison Prevention Campaign

Consider a poison-prevention campaign that includes these precautions:

■ Never take medicines or vitamins in the presence of a young child. They love to imitate.

- Keep labels on medicines, always use child-proof caps, and always keep pharmaceuticals well out of reach of young children—locked in a high cabinet is best. You should also be aware that child-proof caps are not foolproof. At least 15 percent fail each year, and a significant number of poisoning cases involved child-proof caps that either weren't replaced tightly or simply didn't work. Putting "Mr. Yuk" labels on medicines and other no-nos may deter some children, but you should never count on labels alone. Also be aware that an enterprising youngster can easily figure out how to climb on top of a box or stool to reach bureaus or countertops, so lock medicines and other poisons away.
- Carefully discard any old medicine, preferably by flushing it down the toilet.
- Don't ever imply that taking medicine is like eating candy. Since many childhood medications are enhanced with sweet flavors, young children can easily assume they are eating candy, completely unaware they are actually ingesting potentially dangerous drugs.
- Avoid using cleaning products with spicy or fruity scents. Children can mistake that smell for something edible.
- Encourage your children not to eat or drink anything unless it is given to them by an adult.

■ Keep syrup of ipecac handy (to induce vomiting) and activated charcoal (to absorb ingested poisons), though you should never use any antidote without consulting a poison control center. Post the number of the local poison control center near every phone.

## Plants

Many homeowners couldn't imagine a home or yard without plants. Indeed, the sight of greenery can soften the harshest interior environment and give your living space a much more intimate feeling. Unfortunately, some of these decorative plants, especially those that brighten the holidays, also represent a serious risk to young children who don't hesitate to eat almost anything within reach.

How do you avoid problems?

■ Identify house and garden plants; know which are poisonous.
■ Display plants out of reach of your children.
■ Remind your children that plants are not safe to eat.
■ Be ready if there is an emergency: always keep the number of the local poison control center handy.

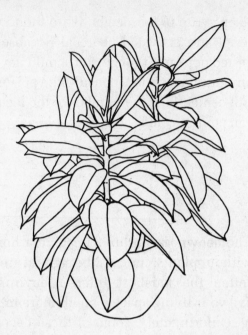

*A rubber plant is an example of a nontoxic plant.*

To help you better identify potential hazards, here's a rundown of the most common problem plants in the home and yard. Remember, though, that poison centers will need to know the scientific name for the plant in question—the common name won't do. The following tables list problem plants with their common names in parentheses if different from the scientific name.

## Which Plants Are Safe?

So much advice you get as a parent seems remarkably similar to the way you sometimes talk to your

## CULTIVATED PLANTS

| Name | Toxic Parts |
| --- | --- |
| *Caladium* | all |
| *Colocasia* (elephant ear, dasheen) | all |
| *Dieffenbachia* (dumb cane) | all |
| *Monstera* (Swiss-cheese plant, ceriman) | all |
| *Philodendron* | all |
| *Caesalpinia gilliesii* (poinciana, bird of paradise) | all |
| *Convallaria majalis* (lily-of-the-valley) | all |
| *Daphne mezereum* (daphne) | all, esp. berries |
| *Delphinium* (larkspur) | all, esp. seeds |
| *Digitalis* (foxglove) | leaves, seeds, flowers |
| *Hedera helix* (English ivy) | all |
| *Hyacinthus orientalis* (hyacinth) | bulb, leaves, flowers |
| *Hydrangea macrophyla* (hydrangea) | leaves, buds |
| *Ilex* spp. (holly) | berries |
| *Ipomoea purpurea* (morning glory) | seeds |
| *Iris* | rootstalk, leaves |
| *Lantana* (wild sage, tea plant) | all, esp. berries |
| *Lathyrus odoratus* (sweet pea) | pea or seed |
| *Ligustrum* spp. (privet, wax-leaf ligustrum) | leaves, berries |
| *Malus sylvestris* (apple) | seeds |
| *Narcissus* (daffodil) | bulb |
| *Nerium oleander* (oleander) | leaves, stems, flowers |
| *Prunus* spp. (peach, plum, cherry, apricot, nectarine) | leaves, stems, bark, pits |
| *Prunus virginiana* (chokecherry) | leaves, stems, bark, pits |

CULTIVATED PLANTS (*continued*)

| Name | Toxic Parts |
| --- | --- |
| *Rheum rhabarbarum* (rhubarb) | leaf |
| *Rhododendron* (azalea) | all *Ricinus communis* (castor bean) | seed, if chewed |
| *Solanum pseudocapsicum* (Jerusalem cherry) | all |
| *Taxus* (yew) | seeds, leaves |
| *Wisteria* | pods, seeds |

children: "Don't, don't, don't." So suppose you enjoy plants but don't particularly like the prospect of poisoning your children? What do you do? Choose plants that aren't particularly toxic. See the list of these on page 140.

## Physical Hazards

According to a study by Baltimore's Johns Hopkins Children's Center, one child in five under the age of fifteen is hurt seriously enough each year to require medical treatment. What's more, accidents are the cause of half the fatalities in the same age group. While those statistics may seem alarming, experts reassure us that many of these accidents can be prevented.

## WILD PLANTS

| Name | Toxic Parts |
| --- | --- |
| *Arisaema triphyllum* (Jack-in-the-pulpit) | leaves |
| *Atropa belladona* (deadly nightshade, belladona) | all |
| *Cicuta maculata* (water hemlock, spotted cowbane) | all |
| *Conium macalatum* (poison hemlock) | all |
| *Datura meteloides* (moonflower, angel's trumpet) | leaves, flowers, seeds |
| *Datura stramonium* (jimsonweed, Thorn apple) | leaf, flowers, seeds |
| *Gelsemium sempervirens* (yellow or Carolina) | all |
| *Parthenocissus quinquefolia* (Virginia creeper, American ivy) | berry, leaf |
| *Phytolacca americana* (pokeweed) | all |
| *Podophyllum peltatum* (May apple, mandrake) | leaf, stem fruit |
| *Robinia pseudoacacia* (black or white locust) | young leaves |
| *Solanum dulcamara* (European bittersweet climbing or deadly nightshade) | leaf, berry |

Source: *The Perfectly Safe Home*

## NONTOXIC PLANTS

### Tall Plants (over five feet):

*Araucaria excelsa* (Norfolk pine)
*Chamaedorea elegans* (parlor palm)
*Ficus benjamina* (small-leaf rubber plant; weeping fig)
*Ficus elastica* (rubber plant)
*Hibiscus rosa-sinensis* (hibiscus, rose-of-China)
*Phyllostachys aurea* (bamboo)

### Medium Plants (one to five feet):

*Asplenium nidus* (bird's nest fern)
*Coleus* species (coleus)
*Crassula argenta* (jade plant)
*Yucca* species (yucca)

### Small Plants (under one foot):

*Aphelandra squarrosa* (zebra plant)
*Echeveria* species (hens and chickens)
*Gynura aurantiaca* (purple passion)
*Saintpaulia ionantha* (African violet)
*Schlumbergera* species (Christmas cactus)

### Plants Suitable for Hanging Baskets

*Asparagus densiflorus* (asparagus fern)
*Cissus rhombifolia* (grape ivy)
*Pellonia daveauana* (watermelon begonia)
*Tradescantia fluminensis* (wandering Jew)

Source: *Baby Safe Houseplants and Cut Flowers*

Infants exhibit an insatiable curiosity that is a natural part of their development. Unfortunately, that curiosity is sometimes the reason for accidents and injuries when those crawling or toddling babies encounter something that SHOULD be out of their reach. The best course is to child-proof your home.

Remember, however, that no two children are alike. While it makes good sense to follow the general guidelines below, you know your child best. There's also no substitute for getting down on all fours—it's fascinating to get your child's perspective!—to spot the particular hazards in your environment. No two homes are ever baby-proofed the same way. One child will always make a beeline to poke his finger into every single one of the electrical outlets; his younger sister may never give them a second glance, heading instead straight for the bathroom to explore the toilet. One child may be a drawer- and cabinet-dumping fiend; another's specialty will be swallowing coins that have rolled off the dresser. You'll never be able to guess how your child's instinctive tastes for putting him or herself in inadvertent jeopardy will change from day to day or minute to minute, so the best course of action is to child-proof as much as possible and stay on the alert. And remember that you'll have to be particularly attentive when visiting other homes, with different—or nonexistent—levels of baby-proofing.

## For All Rooms

First things first: inspect all electrical outlets and cords. Keep all outlets, whether used or unused, covered with child-proof safety caps. You'll need to tailor the style of cap to your own child's ingenuity and motor skill; you'll be amazed at how easily some children can pull the simple caps out of outlets. Coil and tie up any excess electrical cord, then put it out of the child's reach or tape it to the wall or floor to avoid tripping accidents. Some baby-proofing suppliers sell gizmos you can use to store excess cord. Watch out for dangling cords when using appliances such as irons; never leave such appliances unattended for a moment.

Burns are a common hazard for children of all ages. Heaters, obviously, are a potential source of burns, but your crawling baby or careering toddler won't know that. Make certain your space heaters have protective guards. Fireplaces should have metal screens or glass doors. Many radiators can be partially or completely covered to shield the hottest areas.

Needless to say, small children seem to be drawn to these hazards like moths to flame. It may not always work to shout "No, hot!" as they approach them, since the object in question may or may not be hot at the time. It may be better to shout "No, dangerous!" to an inquisitive child so that he or she associates the hazard with danger at all times, not just when it's in operation.

Install smoke detectors in all rooms—or at least one on every floor—and change the batteries in them twice a year; many people do this chore when they adjust their clocks for Daylight Savings Time. Put fire extinguishers on every floor. Develop a fire escape plan for your house, and rehearse it with your older children so they know what to do. Your local fire department can give you special stickers to indicate your children's bedrooms; these will be targeted first during fire rescue. Consider a safety ladder for your home and plan which window you'll use it in if an emergency arises.

For young toddlers, install safety gates at the top and bottom of all stairs. Avoid using the accordion-style gate with V-shaped or diamond-shaped openings along the top; children can get their necks caught in them. Make certain that stair handrails

are secure, and check open balusters on stairways and balconies to make certain the spaces aren't wide enough for a child to squeeze through or catch his or her head in. If they are, consider a barricade of some sort. Many children's catalogs sell netting for this purpose.

While you're checking the spacing of the bars on stairways, don't forget to inspect chairs and other furniture for the same hazard. A beautifully carved piece of furniture could be a choking hazard.

You can buy adjustable gates to declare certain rooms permanently or temporarily off-limits. Many of these can be removed easily for access when the kids aren't around.

Avoid putting your child in a baby walker. They are certainly tempting; most infants love the thrill of being able to navigate themselves through the house at will. However, they give a child added height, allowing him or her to reach things otherwise off-limits. Also, these wheeled walkers give children mobility long before they are ready to understand the hazards they'll encounter, and many take serious tumbles as a result. Both the American Medical Association and the American Academy of Pediatrics have petitioned the Consumer Product Safety Commission to ban the manufacture of the wheeled play seats, citing evidence that more than twenty-nine thousand infants are injured in walkers every year.

One of your most important jobs is to keep small items out of your young children's reach, and remember that adept little ones will find many ways to climb from one object to another until they can get at the object of temptation. I can't emphasize enough that since children have a tendency to put everything in their mouths, you must be especially careful to keep small things out of their reach; probably no other aspect of child-proofing requires more diligence. Stay on the alert for knickknacks, small toys, or pieces from larger toys (an older sibling's toys can be lethal for an infant or toddler), balloons, scissors, coins, and bowls of nuts or candy—all choking hazards. Each house has its own constantly changing hit list of small objects, each its own hazard. Here's where crawling on your hands and knees to get your child's vantage point comes in particularly handy. Also remember that children can pull over heavy objects, so move these out of reach. And make sure shelves are anchored.

Keep the venetian blind and curtain cords on your windows out of reach; children can strangle in them. Put guards on your window so children can't open them too wide or climb out of them and fall.

Make certain all your rugs have slip-resistant backing.

Check all furniture and cabinets to make certain they don't contain anything hazardous. If they do, either clean them out or install child-proof safety

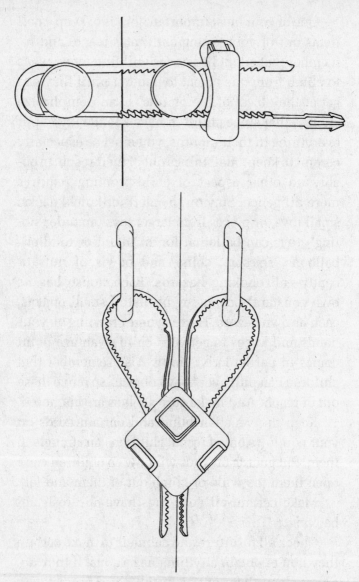

*Different kinds of child-proof safety latches.*

latches. Since many children are inveterately curious about the hidden contents of cabinets, it sometimes helps, particularly in the kitchen, to allow them access to one safe cabinet or drawer that they can open and dump out to their heart's content.

Clear your lower shelves and tables of anything small or breakable. You'll have to raise that yardstick constantly as your child becomes more ingenious at reaching objects higher up.

You can purchase plastic or rubber covers to put on the sharp edges of furniture. If you have a glass coffee table or similar piece of furniture, put bumpers around it.

Never leave exercise equipment out, especially if it contains belts, gears, or pulleys. If you plan to buy exercise gear, find a model that is child-proof, or modify your existing equipment where possible. Schwinn, for example, offers a child-proof chain guard for its older-model exercise bikes.

Consider installing doorknob covers (which children can't turn) on doors to rooms that are off-limits, or install a hook-and-eye latch at your eye level. Be especially cautious about entrances to basements and attics, which typically have unprotected staircases.

Check all door locks to make certain none can be locked from the inside (bathrooms commonly have interior locks). Either remove the lock or tape it so it cannot be engaged. If you want privacy in the bathroom, install a hook-and-eye latch that adults can use but children cannot.

Put plastic or rubber stoppers around the edges of doors so they cannot slam on small fingers.

Plastic bags represent suffocating hazards. Tour every room of the house. Avoid plastic liners for trash and garbage cans within children's reach. (Putting any garbage receptacle within a child's reach is risky—kids love to take garbage out of them and put other objects in.) If you have dry cleaning in plastic bags, either knot the bags tightly at the bottom so that children can't get wrapped up inside them, or better yet, remove them completely and discard.

If you have decorative partitions or screens, consider storing them until your child is older. Children don't realize they aren't real walls and often try to lean on them for support.

Once you've taken these general safety steps, consider a room-by-room assessment. Individual rooms pose their own special risks.

### Keeping the Kitchen Safe

Install a guard on your kitchen stove so that little hands can't reach up to fiddle with the knobs or touch the burners. Get into the habit of cooking on the back burners of the stove whenever possible. Always make certain that pan handles are turned in so children can't grab them and pull boiling hot food on top of themselves. Be aware that children may try to push chairs or stepstools over to forbidden areas. Better yet, gate off the kitchen if possible.

If you have a microwave oven, make certain it's situated where curious hands can't punch the buttons or put stray objects inside. Push the coffeemaker back to the wall so your child won't reach up to play with the buttons.

Teach your children never to use the oven or microwave without adult supervision. I know one very bright five-year-old who, unbeknownst to her parents, took some pudding out of the refrigerator, put it in the microwave, and set the timer for ninety-nine minutes. It was not a pretty sight.

Unplug countertop appliances when not in use.

Keep all sharp utensils locked in a child-proof drawer or cabinet or otherwise out of reach. When you have them out, never lay them on a counter where a child could reach them.

Install locks or child-proof safety latches on all cupboards and drawers within a child's reach. Installing these latches is really a very simple affair, and using them is only a very minor annoyance, so there's no reason not to do it.

Store plastic bags—potential suffocation hazards—out of reach.

Keep wastebaskets and garbage cans covered or out of reach.

Keep foods like beans, popcorn, raisins, and nuts out of reach. These are all choking hazards.

Make certain you place highchairs so the toddler's hands or feet can't reach cabinets, tables, or other furniture.

Make certain all booster seats are securely anchored.

### Keeping the Bathroom Safe

*Never, ever* leave a child who is under age four in the bathroom unattended; he or she could easily fall into a full tub or toilet and drown. Keep everything you'll need for a bath—towels, washcloths, shampoo, soap, etc.—within reach and double-check before you put your child in the tub. If your child is bathing and the phone rings or the doorbell chimes and you must answer it, wrap your child in a towel and take him or her with you. Your pediatrician can tell you when your child is old enough to bathe alone. Even if an older sibling is old enough to bathe alone, never let him or her bathe unsupervised with a younger sibling.

Put a lock on your toilet. Stores sell latches that are simple enough for older children to manage but too strong for smaller fingers to pry open. Children can drown in toilets. They also love to drop your precious objects—keys, makeup, coins—in the bowl.

Set your hot water heater so the temperature at

the tap can't exceed 120 degrees. Or install an ac-tuator—a device that senses too-hot water and shuts off the tap immediately. Actuators are available at most hardware stores.

All bathroom cabinets should have locks or child-safe latches. Never store medication in a place reachable by children—even if locks are installed. Studies show that bathrooms—typically warm and humid—aren't the best place to store medications anyway. Be aware that many children can reach the medicine cabinet easily by climbing from the toilet lid to the sink.

Store electrical appliances—hairdryers, shavers, toothbrushes, waterpicks, and the like—so they cannot be pulled into the bathtub or sink. Unplug them when they're not in use. Ask an electrician to install ground fault circuit interrupters (GFCIs) in your bathroom. These will stop the electrical current if an appliance falls into the tub or sink.

Put a nonskid mat in the bathtub. Cover the spout so a child can't hit his or her head on the bare metal. Many stores carry foam and plastic covers for this purpose.

Never keep glass in the bathroom. If you need a cup for drinking, use one made of plastic or paper.

As mentioned above, inventory all the hazardous products usually kept in bathrooms and make certain they're locked away or stored out of reach.

## Keeping Your Basement and Garage Safe

As mentioned earlier, keep potentially harmful products or power tools out of reach.

Put a lock on basement and shed doors.

Disconnect the spark plug from your gasoline-powered mower when it's not in use.

Make certain your automatic garage door opener has an automatic reverse features that activates whenever the door encounters resistance. The Consumer Product Safety Commission says that several dozen children are killed each year by automatic garage doors.

Never let children play in or around unattended parked cars.

Give every item in these locations a close inspection. Do you have sharp barbecue tools that could poke? Lots of loose nuts and bolts that could be swallowed?

## Keeping the Nursery Safe

When buying new furniture, buggies, or strollers, make certain each item has been certified by the Juvenile Products Manufacturing Association. An association seal means that the product meets approved safety standards. Be wary of hand-me-downs, garage sale bargains, or family heirlooms. They might be beautiful, but they may have been made before current laws ensured their safety. Watch for crib bars that are so widely spaced that they would permit a child's head to get caught, or old paint that might contain lead.

Check windows to make certain the latches work. If you have sliding windows, install latches that limit the size of the opening.

Make certain the door can't be locked from the inside.

Put firefighter alert stickers on outside windows—as long as they're approved by your local fire department.

Have your children wear flame-retardant sleepwear.

For infants younger than four months, keep all objects that could cause smothering out of the crib, including large stuffed animals, heavy blankets, and pillows.

Make certain that any mobiles above the crib are securely attached and lightweight, so in the event they do fall, they will be unlikely to cause great harm. Mobiles should also be removed when the child can stand and reach them.

Check all stuffed animals, small toys, and mobiles to make certain they have no small parts that could be chewed off, swallowed, and choked on. Many children suck or chew on their toys absentmindedly as they're drifting off to sleep.

Consider a nursery monitor or intercom if the nursery is out of hearing range. This item can bring you great peace of mind, and you'll be alert to any suspicious sounds.

Use a changing table with a restraining strap or a V-shaped changing pad. You'd be amazed at how quickly an infant can roll off otherwise—and often there's no hint that newfound ability until the instant it happens. As an added precaution, make certain there's a rug or carpet under the changing table or crib to cushion any fall. If you're at all nervous, just change the baby on the floor.

If you use a vaporizer or humidifier, fill it with distilled water to avoid contaminants found in some water supplies. Water left sitting in a vaporizer can collect molds or funguses that will be dispersed with the steam.

Use only those nightlights with covered bulbs.

## Keeping the Playroom Safe

Toys are a fun part of most children's lives. However, they also represent one of the greatest potential hazards to their welfare. Between January 1, 1993, and September 30, 1994, according to reports made to the Consumer Product Safety Commission, thirty-seven children, aged six months to twelve years, died from toy-related injuries. Most of those deaths were caused by choking on small parts. During that same period, over 130,000 children had to go to emergency rooms to be treated for injuries caused by toys.

Until now, federal law specified only that toys with small parts could not be marketed to children under the age of three; hence the warning on so much packaging that the toy is intended "for children ages 3 and up." As of January 1, 1995, however, a stricter law has gone into effect. It specifies that in addition to the previous marketing ban, the manufacturers of all toys with small parts made or shipped after January 1, 1995, must clearly and explicitly be labeled as choking hazards and state that they require adult supervision. Any toy or game that contains small parts and that is designed for children ages three to six must contain a "clear and noticeable" warning label stating the hazard and be accompanied by a warning symbol (an exclamation mark inside a triangle).

In these days, when the buzzword is "developmentally appropriate," you may be tempted to ignore warning labels by age if you think your child is particularly bright and adept. Perhaps you feel proud that your three-year-old can master a toy that the box states if "for children ages five and up." But you should be aware that these warning labels have nothing to do with your child's intelligence. The Consumer Product Safety Commission isn't thinking about the size of your child's brain; they care about the size of his or her windpipe, and the warning is intended to help you avoid objects that can get stuck in that throat. That means avoiding too-small toys and toy parts no matter how smart your child is.

In addition to the warning about toy parts, you should know that according to the Child Safety Protection Act, balls and marbles smaller than 1.75 inches in diameter cannot be marketed to children under three, who could accidentally swallow them and choke.

As I mentioned earlier, one of the greatest challenges of keeping small objects away from little mouths is keeping an older sibling's toys—such as Legos and other tiny building toys—away from a curious younger sibling. Another hazard, as I mentioned earlier, is balloons. Most children adore them, yet if deflated balloons or popped balloon fragments are inhaled, they can cause grave injury, including brain damage from oxygen deprivation, and death. If your child's birthday wouldn't be the same without balloons, consider ones made of Mylar, which don't pose the same hazard.

When you're storing toys, choose a toy chest with a slow-closing mechanism so children don't get their fingers pinched. The chest shouldn't be airtight, in case a child gets closed inside. As I mentioned earlier, make certain it isn't decorated with lead-based paint.

When considering toys for your child, the best rule is common sense. I don't have to tell you the hazards posed by toys that have sharp points or that go bang or boom. If you have questions about which toys pose hazards, call the Consumer Product

Safety Commission's hotline at (800) 638-2772. If it's difficult for you to determine whether objects pose a choking risk, you can send away for a small cylinder designed by the Consumer Product Safety Commission and also available in toy stores and pharmacies. If the object can fit past the ring inside the cylinder, it's too small for a child under the age of three to play with.

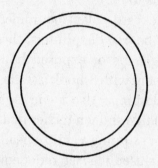

## Safety Outdoors

Always use car safety seats for all children under the age of five. Always use seat belts and/or shoulder restraints for older children.

Place child-height stickers on all sliding glass doors to prevent accidental collisions. Make certain that the glass on all such doors is certified safety glass, which beads on impact instead of shattering into shards.

If you have a backyard pool, fence it and install a lock on the gate. Some child safety catalogs advertise pool alarms that sound if anyone enters the water; I don't think these are any substitute for constant adult supervision.

Locate outdoor grills in a safe place inaccessible to children. Remember that charcoal-fired grills can stay hot for hours. Keep children away from sharp barbecue tools.

Select backyard play equipment carefully. Wood should be free of splinters; there should be no protruding nails or exposed bolts or screws. Avoid equipment with S-hook fasteners, which can easily snag clothing. Also avoid swing sets with rings between five and ten inches in diameter—the perfect size for trapping a child's head. Be cautious about buying a used playset; older equipment may not conform to today's safety standards. Firmly anchor all equipment according to the manufacturer's instructions and install it above a forgiving surface such as sand or wood chips.

If you have a sandbox, cover it when not in use. Otherwise, it will make an attractive litter box for pets and wild animals. Replace the sand inside the box at least once a year. Use only sterilized sand intended specifically for play. Some white, powdery construction sands may contain substances that pose health risks.

When children start using roller skates, in-line skates, and bicycles, see that they wear appropriate protective gear, particularly safety-approved helmets.

When you take your child shopping, belt him or her into the shopping cart if possible. Carts can tip easily if children stand up in them.

## Other Precautions

Keep the numbers of the nearest poison control center, fire department, police department, and your pediatrician posted next to all phones. When your child is old enough, teach him or her to dial 911 in an emergency. Have your child memorize your address and phone number as soon as he or she is able.

Keep a basic first aid book on hand. Consider taking a basic adult/infant CPR and emergency care course, and take refresher courses as needed. Check with your local Red Cross chapter or hospital for information on classes.

Keep a well-stocked first aid kit in the house, and another smaller kit in each car. The ideal household kit will include the usual assortment of bandages, gauze patches, tape, and medicinal ointments along with:

- Syrup of ipecac, to be used to induce vomiting after a poisoning. Use only after you've been given the go-ahead from the poison control center

■ Activated charcoal, to absorb ingested poisons. Use only on the advice of the poison control center

■ Antihistamine, an antidote for allergic reactions to insect stings, etc. (ask your pediatrician to recommend a brand)

■ Calamine lotion

■ Tweezers

■ Hydrogen peroxide

■ Rubbing alcohol

■ Children's aspirin or nonaspirin substitute (as your pediatrician recommends)

■ Tourniquet

■ Disposable ice bag

■ Thermometer

Most baby- and child-proofing comes down to common sense.

## CHECKLIST

❏ Scour your house for potentially toxic substances. Keep them out of children's reach and substitute nontoxic materials whenever possible.

❏ Start your own poison prevention campaign at home.

❑ Determine which, if any, of your houseplants is poisonous. Keep hazardous ones out of reach. Better
yet, buy nontoxic plants to replace them.

❑ Perform a room-by-room check to child-proof your
home.

❑ Take a child and infant CPR/baby safety course.

❑ Keep a basic first aid book on hand.

❑ Prepare a well-stocked first aid kit and keep it
handy.

❑ Post the names of your local poison control center,
fire department, police department, and pediatrician next to all phones.

## RESOURCES

### Mail Order for Home Safety Equipment

The Safety Zone
Hanover, PA 17333-0019

Perfectly Safe
7245 Whipple Ave NW
North Canton, OH 44720

## Publications

*Baby-Safe Houseplants and Cut Flowers,* John and Dolores Alber, Genus Books, 1990. Available from Perfectly Safe, 7245 Whipple Avenue NW, North Canton, OH 44720, (800) 837-KIDS.

*Guide to Hazardous Products Around the Home,* Household Hazardous Waste Project, 901 South National Avenue, Box 87, Springfield, MO 65804, (417) 836-5777.

*Nontoxic and Natural: How to Avoid Dangerous Everyday Products.* Available at stores or directly from the author: Debra Lynn Dodd, Box 1506, Mill Valley, CA 94942.

*The Perfectly Safe Home,* Jeanne Miller, Simon & Schuster, 1991.

*Stepping Lightly on the Earth: Everyone's Guide to Toxics in the Home,* Greenpeace, 1436 U Street NW, Suite 201A, Washington, DC 20009, (202) 462-8817.

*TIPP: The Injury Prevention Program,* a brochure available from the American Academy of Pediatrics, Division of Publications, 141 Northwest Point Boulevard, Box 927, Elk Grove Village, IL 60009.

# RESOURCES

The federal Environmental Protection Agency and the appropriate state agency have offices to help answer your questions about the environment in your community. Here are the locations and phone numbers for those offices.

## U.S. Environmental Protection Agency Regional Offices

REGION 1
(Connecticut, Maine, Massachusetts, New Hampshire, Rhode Island, Vermont)
JFK Federal Building
Boston, MA 02203
(617) 565-4939

REGION 2
(New York, New Jersey, Puerto Rico, Virgin Islands)
2890 Woodbridge Avenue, Building 10
Edison, NJ 08837
(908) 906-6890

REGION 3
(Delaware, District of Columbia, Maryland, Pennsylvania, Virginia, West Virginia)
841 Chestnut Building
Philadelphia, PA 19107
(215) 597-3156

REGION 4
(Alabama, Florida, Georgia, Kentucky, Mississippi, North Carolina, South Carolina, Tennessee)
345 Courtland Street NE
Atlanta, GA 30365
(404) 347-1033

REGION 5
(Illinois, Indiana, Michigan, Minnesota, Ohio, Wisconsin)
77 West Jackson Boulevard
Chicago, IL 60604
(312) 886-6219

REGION 6
(Arkansas, Louisiana, New Mexico, Oklahoma, Texas)
1445 Dallas Avenue, Suite 700
Dallas, TX 75202

REGION 7
(Iowa, Kansas, Missouri, Nebraska)
726 Minnesota Avenue
Kansas City, KS 66101
(913) 551-7472

REGION 8
(Colorado, Montana, North Dakota, South Dakota, Utah,
   Wyoming)
999 18th Street, Suite 500
Denver, CO 80202
(303) 293-1229

REGION 9
(Arizona, California, Hawaii, Nevada, American Samoa,
   Guam, Northern Marianas)
75 Hawthorne Street
San Francisco, CA 94105
(415) 744-1116

REGION 10
(Alaska, Idaho, Oregon, Washington)
1200 Sixth Avenue
Seattle, WA 98101
(206) 553-8338

## State Agencies

ALABAMA
Department of Environmental Management
1751 Congressman W. L. Dickinson Drive
Montgomery, AL 36109
(205) 260-2717

ALASKA
Department of Environmental Conservation
410 Willoughby, Suite 105
Juneau, AK 99801
(907) 465-5220

ARIZONA
Emergency Response Commission
5636 East McDowell Road
Phoenix, AZ 85008
(602) 231-6346

ARKANSAS
Department of Pollution Control and Ecology
8001 National Drive
Little Rock, AR 72209
(501) 562-7444

CALIFORNIA
Environmental Protection Agency
555 Capitol Mall, Suite 525
Sacramento, CA 95814
(916) 324-9924

COLORADO
Department of Health
4300 Cherry Creek Drive South
Denver, CO 80222
(303) 692-3017

CONNECTICUT
Department of Environmental Protection
79 Elm Street
Hartford, CT 06106
(203) 424-3373

DELAWARE
Department of Natural Resources and Environmental Control
89 Kings Highway
P.O. Box 1401
Dover, DE 19903
(302) 739-4791

DISTRICT OF COLUMBIA
Office of Emergency Preparedness
Frank Reeves Center for Municipal Affairs
2000 14th Street NW
Washington, DC 20009
(202) 727-6161

FLORIDA
Emergency Response Commission
2740 Centerview Drive
Tallahassee, FL 32399
(904) 413-9929

GEORGIA
Emergency Response Commission
205 Butler Street SE
Floyd Tower East, Suite 1166
Atlanta, GA 30334
(404) 656-6905

HAWAII
Department of Health
P.O. Box 3378
Honolulu, HI 96801
(808) 586-4694

IDAHO
Emergency Response Commission
1109 Main Street
State House
Boise, ID 83720
(208) 334-3253

ILLINOIS
Environmental Protection Agency
Office of Chemical Safety
P.O. Box 19276
2200 Churchill Road

Springfield, IL 62794
(217) 785-0830

INDIANA
Emergency Response Commission
5500 West Bradbury Avenue
Indianapolis, IN 46241
(317) 232-8172

IOWA
Department of Natural Resources
Wallace Office Building
900 East Grand Avenue
Des Moines, IA 50319
(515) 281-8852

KANSAS
Emergency Response Commission
Forbes Field Building 283
Topeka, KS 66620
(913) 296-1690

KENTUCKY
Department for Environmental Protection
14 Reilly Road
Franfort, KY 40601
(502) 564-2150

LOUISIANA
Department of Environmental Quality
P.O. Box 82263
Baton Rouge, LA 70884
(504) 765-0737

MAINE
Department of Environmental Protection
Statehouse Station 17

Augusta, ME 04333
(800) 452-1942

MARYLAND
Department of the Environment
2500 Broening Highway
Baltimore, MD 21224
(410) 631-3800

MASSACHUSETTS
Department of Environmental Protection
1 Winter Street
Boston, MA 02108
(617) 292-5500

MICHIGAN
Department of Natural Resources
Environmental Response Division
P.O. Box 30028
Lansing, MI 48909
(517) 373-8481

MINNESOTA
Emergency Response Commission
B5 State Capitol Building
St. Paul, MN 55155
(612) 282-5396

MISSISSIPPI
Emergency Management Agency
P.O. Box 4501
Jackson, MS 39296
(601) 960-9000

MISSOURI
Department of Natural Resources
P.O. Box 176

Jefferson City, MO 65102
(314) 526-6627

MONTANA
Emergency Response Commission
Cogswell Building A-107, Capitol Station
Helena, MT 59620
(406) 444-2544

NEBRASKA
Department of Environmental Quality
P.O. Box 98922
Lincoln, NE 68509
(402) 471-4230

NEVADA
Division of Environmental Protection
333 West Nye Lane
Capitol Complex
Carson City, NV 89710
(702) 687-5872

NEW HAMPSHIRE
Office of Emergency Management
State Office Park South
107 Pleasant Street
Concord, NH 03301
(603) 271-2231

NEW JERSEY
Department of Environmental Protection and Energy
Bureau of Hazardous Substances Information
401 East State Street
Trenton, NJ 08625
(609) 984-3219

NEW MEXICO
Emergency Response Commission
Chemical Safety Office
P.O. Box 1628
Santa Fe, NM 87504
(505) 827-9223

NEW YORK
Department of Environmental Conservation
Room 340
50 Wolf Road
Albany, NY 12233
(518) 457-4107

NORTH CAROLINA
Emergency Response Commission
116 West Jones Street
Raleigh, NC 27603
(919) 733-3865

NORTH DAKOTA
Division of Emergency Management
P.O. Box 5511
Bismark, ND 58502
(701) 328-2111

OHIO
Division of Air Pollution Control
1800 Watermark Drive
Columbus, OH 43215
(614) 644-4830

OKLAHOMA
Department of Environmental Quality
1000 Northeast Tenth Street
Oklahoma City, OK 73117
(405) 271-8062

OREGON
Emergency Response Commission
4760 Portland Road NE
Salem, OR 97305
(503) 378-3473 Ext. 231

PENNSYLVANIA
Emergency Management Council
Room 1503
Labor and Industry Building
Seventh and Forster Streets
Harrisburg, PA 17120
(717) 783-2071

RHODE ISLAND
Department of Environmental Management
Division of Air and Hazardous Materials
291 Promenade Street
Providence, RI 02908
(401) 277-2808

SOUTH CAROLINA
Department of Health and Environmental Control
2600 Bull Street
Columbia, SC 29201
(803) 896-4117

SOUTH DAKOTA
Department of Environment and Natural Resources
Joe Foss Building
523 East Capitol
Pierre, SD 57501
(605) 773-3296

TENNESSEE
Emergency Management Agency
3041 Sidco Drive

Nashville, TN 37204
(615) 741-2986

Texas
Natural Resources Conservation Commission
P.O. Box 13807
Austin, TX 78711
(512) 239-3100

Utah
Hazardous Chemical Emergency Response Commission
P.O. Box 144840
Salt Lake City, UT 84116
(801) 536-4100

Vermont
Pollution Prevention and Education Division
103 South Main Street
West Office Building
Waterbury, VT 05671
(802) 241-3888

Virginia
Department of Environmental Quality
Ninth Floor
P.O. Box 10009
Richmond, VA 23240
(804) 762-4482

Washington
Department of Ecology
P.O. Box 47659
Olympia, WA 98504
(206) 407-6727

West Virginia
Emergency Response Commission
Main Capitol Building 1

Room EB-80
Charleston, WV 25305
(304) 558-5380

WISCONSIN
Department of Natural Resources
101 South Webster
P.O. Box 7921
Madison, WI 53707
(608) 266-9255

WYOMING
Emergency Response Commission
P.O. Box 1709
Cheyenne, WY 82003
(307) 777-4900

## Regional Poison Control Centers

ALABAMA

Children's Hospital of Alabama
1600 Seventh Avenue South
Birmingham, AL 35233
Hotline: (205) 939-9201; 933-4050; (800) 292-6678

Alabama Poison Center
408-A Paul Bryant Drive East
Tuscaloosa, AL 35401
(205) 345-0600; (800) 462-0800

ARIZONA

Arizona Poison & Drug Information Center
Arizona Health Sciences Center, Room 3204K
University of Arizona
1501 North Campbell Avenue

Tucson, AZ 85724
(602) 626-6016; (800) 362-0101

Samaritan Regional Poison Center
1441 North Twelfth Street
Phoenix, AZ 85006
(602) 253-3334

CALIFORNIA

Central California Regional Poison Control Center
Valley Children's Hospital
3151 North Millbrook
Fresno, CA 93703
(209) 445-1222; (800) 346-5922

Santa Clara Valley Regional Poison Center
Valley Health Center
Suite 310
750 South Bascom Avenue
San Jose, CA 95128
(408) 885-6000; (800) 662-9886

San Diego Regional Poison Center
UCSD Medical Center
225 Dickinson Street
San Diego, CA 92103
(619) 543-6000; (800) 876-4766

San Francisco Bay Area Regional Poison Control Center
San Francisco General Hospital
Room 1E86
1001 Potrero Avenue
San Francisco, CA 94110
(800) 523-2222

UCDMC Regional Poison Control Center
2315 Stockton Boulevard
Sacramento, CA 95817
(916) 734-3692; (800) 342-9293

COLORADO

Rocky Mountain Poison and Drug Center
645 Bannock Street
Denver, CO 80204
(303) 629-1123

DISTRICT OF COLUMBIA

National Capital Poison Center
3201 New Mexico Avenue NW
Suite 310
Washington, DC 20016
(202) 625-3333

FLORIDA

Florida Poison Information Center
Tampa General Hospital
P.O. Box 1289
Tampa, FL 33601
(813) 253-444; (800) 282-3171

Florida Poison Information Center-Jacksonville
University Medical Center
University of Florida Health Science Center
655 West Eighth Street
Jacksonville, FL 32209
(904) 549-4480; (800) 282-3171

GEORGIA

Georgia Poison Control Center
Grady Memorial Hospital
Box 26066
80 Butler Street SE
Atlanta, GA 30335
(404) 616-9000; (800) 282-5846

INDIANA

Indiana Poison Center
Methodist Hospital of Indiana
P.O. Box 1367
1701 North Senate Boulevard
Indianapolis, IN 46206
(317) 929-2323; (800) 382-9097

KENTUCKY

Kentucky Regional Poison Center
Children's Hospital
P.O. Box 35070
Louisville, KY 40232
(502) 629-7275; (800) 722-5725

MARYLAND

Maryland Poison Center
20 North Pine Street
Baltimore, MD 21201
(301) 528-7701; (800) 492-2414

National Capital Poison Center (D.C. suburbs only)
3201 New Mexico Avenue NW
Suite 310
Washington, DC 20016
(202) 625-3333

MASSACHUSETTS

Massachusetts Poison Control System
300 Longwood Avenue
Boston, MA 02115
(617) 232-2120; (800) 682-9211

MICHIGAN

Poison Control Center
Children's Hospital of Michigan

3901 Beaubien Boulevard
Detroit, MI 48210
(313) 745-5711

MINNESOTA

Hennepin Regional Poison Center
Hennepin County Medical Center
701 Park Avenue
Minneapolis, MN 55415
(612) 347-3141

Minnesota Regional Poison Center
St. Paul–Ramsey Medical Center
640 Jackson Street
St. Paul, MN 55101
(612) 221-2113

MISSOURI

Cardinal Glennon Children's Hospital Regional Poison Center
1465 South Grand Boulevard
St. Louis, MO 63104
(314) 772-5200; (800) 366-8888

MONTANA

Rocky Mountain Regional Poison and Drug Center
645 Bannock Street
Denver, CO 80204
(303) 629-1123

NEBRASKA

Mid-Plains Poison Control Center
8301 Dodge Street
Omaha, NE 68114
(402) 390-5555; (800) 955-9119 (NE & WY)

NEW JERSEY

New Jersey Poison Information and Education System
201 Lyons Avenue
Newark, NJ 07112
(800) 962-1253

NEW MEXICO

New Mexico Poison and Drug Information Center
University of New Mexico
Albuquerque, NM 87131
(505) 843-2551; (800) 432-6866

NEW YORK

Long Island Regional Poison Control Center
Nassau County Medical Center
2201 Hempstead Turnpike
East Meadow, NY 11554
(516) 542-2323

New York City Poison Control Center
455 First Avenue
Room 123
New York, NY 10016
(212) 340-4494

Hudson Valley Regional Poison Center
Phelps Memorial Hospital Center
701 North Broadway
North Tarrytown, NY 10591
(914) 366-3030

NORTH CAROLINA

Carolinas Poison Center
100 Blythe Boulevard
Charlotte, NC 28232
(704) 355-4000

OHIO

Central Ohio Poison Center
Columbus Children's Hospital
700 Children's Drive
Columbus, OH 43205
(614) 461-2012

Regional Poison Control System
Cincinnati Drug and Poison Information Center
231 Bethesda Avenue
Cincinnati, OH 45267
(513) 558-5111; (800) 872-5111

OREGON

Oregon Poison Center
Oregon Health Sciences University
3181 Sam Jackson Park Road
Portland, OR 97201
(503) 494-8968; (800) 462-7165

PENNSYLVANIA

Delaware Valley Regional Poison Control Center
One Children's Center
34th & Civic Center Boulevard
Philadelphia, PA 19104
(215) 386-2100

Pittsburgh Poison Center
3705 Fifth Avenue
Pittsburgh, PA 15213
(412) 681-6669

Central Pennsylvania Poison Center
University Hospital
Milton South Hershey Medical Center

Hershey, PA 17033
(800) 521-6110

RHODE ISLAND

Rhode Island Poison Center
Rhode Island Hospital
593 Eddy Street
Providence, RI 02902
(401) 444-5727

TEXAS

North Texas Poison Center
P.O. Box 35926
Dallas, TX 75235
(214) 590-5000; (800) 441-0040

Texas State Poison Center
The University of Texas Medical Branch
Galveston, TX 77550
(409) 765-1420 (Galveston); (713) 654-1701 (Houston)

UTAH

Utah Poison Control Center
5410 Chipeta Way
Suite 230
Salt Lake City, UT 84108
(801) 581-2151; (800) 456-7707

VIRGINIA

Blue Ridge Poison Center
Box 67
Blue Ridge Hospital
Charlottesville, VA 22901
(804) 924-5543; (800) 451-1428

National Capital Poison Center (North Virginia only)
3201 New Mexico Avenue NW
Suite 310
Washington, DC 20016
(202) 625-3333

WEST VIRGINIA

West Virginia Poison Center
West Virginia University Health Sciences Center
3110 MacCorkle Avenue SE
Charleston, WV 25304
(304) 348-4211; (800) 642-3625

WYOMING

The Poison Center
8301 Dodge Street
Omaha, NE 68114
(800) 955-9119

## Other Government Agencies

Food and Drug Administration
Consumer Communications HFE-88
Rockville, MD 20857
(Has a helpful brochure on childhood poison prevention.)

Centers for Disease Control
Atlanta, GA
(404) 488-7300

Consumer Product Safety Commission
Washington, DC 20207
(800) 638-2772
(Has helpful brochures on toys, swimming pools, electrical risks, sports equipment, and a host of other consumer products.)

National Institute of Environmental Health Sciences
P.O. Box 12233
Research Triangle Park, NC 27709
(919) 541-3345
(This is the principal federal research center for issues related to environmental risks.)

## Health/Environment Organizations

Alliance to End Childhood Lead Poisoning
227 Massachusetts Avenue NE
Washington, DC 20002
(202) 543-1147
(A nonprofit advocacy group that parents can turn to for additional information on issues related to lead contamination.)

American Cancer Society
1599 Clifton Road NE
Atlanta, GA 30329
(404) 329-7686

American Lung Association
1726 M Street NW
Suite 902
Washington, DC 20036
(202) 785-3355
(Has brochures and a videotape on household air quality.)

League of Conservation Voters
1730 M Street NW
Washington, DC 20036
(202) 429-1965
(A nonpartisan political group that offers excellent brochures on water quality and on household pesticides, poisons.)

Mothers and Others for a Livable Planet
40 West Twentieth Street
New York, NY 10011
(212) 727-4474
(National group involved in issues related to childhood environmental risks with a special emphasis on pesticides in foods.)

# INDEX

RAE TYSON, a veteran journalist, is an environmental reporter and editor at *USA Today*. Tyson began his journalism career at the Niagara *Gazette* in Niagara Falls, New York, where he covered the Love Canal disaster. Winner of numerous journalism awards, Tyson has traveled extensively throughout the world to cover major environmental stories. Prior to his career in journalism, Tyson taught science at both the public school and college level. He lives in Virginia with his wife, Joan, two children, Mariah and Peter, two cats, a dog and a hamster.